Music Makes the Difference ®

Music Makes the Difference®

Music, Brain Development, and Learning

The National Association for Music Education

CONTENTS

Foreword vii

Advocacy

Talking Points 2
Ardene Shafer and Michael Blakeslee

Straight Talk about Music and Brain Research 10
Ella Wilcox

Research Linking Music and Intelligence: Helpful or
Harmful to the String Teaching Profession 16
Laura Reed Racin

Music and Young Children

Lessons of the Music Womb 30
Norman M. Weinberger

Recent Brain Research on Young Children 37
John Flohr, Daniel C. Miller, and Diane C. Persellin

The Effect of Music Training on Preschoolers' Spatial-
Temporal Task Performance 44
Joyce Eastlund Gromko and Allison Smith Poorman

Academic Achievement

SAT Scores of Students in the Arts
Sue Rarus 56

The Effects of Three Years of Piano Instruction on
Children's Cognitive Development 58
Eugenia Costa-Giomi

Involvement in the Arts and Human Development: General
Involvement and Intensive Involvement in Music
and Theater Arts 74
James S. Catterall

The Intrinsic Value of Music Education

Growing Up Complete: The Imperative for Music
Education 104
National Commission on Music Education

Facing the Risks of the "Mozart Effect" 118
  Bennett Reimer

Resources

Annotated Bibliography: Music, Brain Development,
  and Learning 134
  Wendy L. Sims and Cathi C. Wilson

Web sites 142
  Sue Rarus

This collection of essays, studies, and resources provides varied and convincing arguments about the value of music education. Many of these essays have appeared in well-known educational periodicals and research journals. Up-to-date information on print and on-line resources related to music, brain development, and learning is also included.

"Advocacy," the first section, offers suggestions for communicating music's value to members of your school, local community, and state and national governments. Recent research linking music and intelligence is summarized.

The second section of the book, "Music and Young Children," looks at the positive relationship between music and children's cognitive development. A key study on the effect of music training on preschoolers' spatial-temporal task performance is included.

In the third section, "Academic Achievement," the strong correlations between music study and academic achievement are discussed. An in-depth study of the positive outcomes of students' involvement in music and theater arts is included.

"The Intrinsic Value of Music Education" is the focus of the fourth section, which offers philosophical discussions about music's inherent value and its many nonquantifiable benefits. Cautions about misusing recent research results are offered.

An annotated bibilography and Web site listings are provided in the final section, "Resources." The bibliography includes resources in three categories: data-based research published in scientific or psychological journals, articles in professional journals, and articles in the popular press. Under the data-based research journals, brief summaries of each article are offered.

This collection of essays is the second book in the *Music Makes the Difference* series. The first book, *Music Makes the Difference: Programs and Partnerships,* described music programs that have flourished as a result of music teachers' creativity and cooperation with community groups, businesses, and local colleges. This new book, *Music Makes the Difference: Music, Brain Development, and Learning*, provides equally important information, which can be used in efforts to maintain quality music programs and promote music education.

—The MENC Editors

Advocacy

Talking Points

Ardene Shafer and Michael Blakeslee

The talking points included here were presented at MENC's National Assembly in July 1999 in Reston, Virginia. This information, which supports the value of music education, is meant to be disseminated to parents, school officials, community members, and local and national government leaders. This information is also located on the MENC Web site (www.menc.org) in a section called "Facts and Figures."

"Every student in the nation should have an education in the arts." This is the opening statement of "The Value and Quality of Arts Education: A Statement of Principles," a document from the nation's ten most important education organizations, including the American Association of School Administrators, the National Education Association, the National PTA, and the National School Boards Association.

The basic statement is unlikely to be challenged by anyone involved in education. In the sometimes harsh reality of limited time and funding for instruction, however, the inclusion of the arts in every student's education can sometimes be relegated to a distant wish rather than an exciting reality.

It doesn't have to be that way.

All that is needed is a clear message, clearly sent to all those who must make the hard choices involved in running a school or school system. It is the purpose of this document to marshal the most convincing arguments for arts education—specifically, for music education—so that advocates for this essential part of each student's experience can present a uniform message to decision-makers.

The benefits conveyed by music education can be grouped in four categories:

- Success in society
- Success in school
- Success in developing intelligence
- Success in life

We firmly believe that, presented with the many manifest benefits of music education, officials at all levels will universally support a full, balanced, sequential course of music instruction taught by qualified teachers.

And every student *will* have an education in the arts.

Benefit One: Success in Society

Perhaps the basic reason why every child must have an education in music is that music is a part of the fabric of our society. The intrinsic value of music for each individual is widely recognized in the many cultures that make up American life—indeed, every human culture uses music to carry forward its ideas and ideals. The importance of music to our economy is without doubt. And the value of music in shaping individual abilities and character is attested in a number of places:

- The U.S. Department of Education lists the arts as subjects that college-bound middle and junior high school students should take, stating "Many colleges view participation in the arts and music as a valuable experience that broadens students' understanding and appreciation of the world around them. It is also well known and widely recognized that the arts contribute significantly to children's intellectual development." In addition, one year of Visual and Performing Arts is recommended for college-bound high school students.—*Getting Ready for College Early: A Handbook for Parents of Students in the Middle and Junior High School Years, U.S. Department of Education, 1997*

- The College Board identifies the arts as one of the six basic academic subject areas students should study in order to succeed in college.—*Academic Preparation for College: What Students Need to Know and Be Able to Do, 1983 [still in use], The College Board, New York*

- The arts create jobs, increase the local tax base, boost tourism, spur growth in related businesses (hotels, restaurants, printing, etc.) and improve the overall quality of life for our cities and towns. On a national level, nonprofit arts institutions and organizations generate an estimated $37 billion in economic activity and return $3.4 billion in federal income taxes to the U.S. Treasury each year.—*American Arts Alliance Fact Sheet, October 1996*

- The very best engineers and technical designers in the Silicon Valley industry are, nearly without exception, practicing musicians.— *Grant Venerable, "The Paradox of the Silicon Savior," as reported in "The Case for Sequential Music Education in the Core Curriculum of the Public Schools," The Center for the Arts in the Basic Curriculum, New York, 1989*
- "To compete effectively in today's rapidly changing business climate, a firm must have employees who can think creatively and work productively in a team environment. Arts education facilitates development of those skills more effectively than most classes in traditional "basic" subjects. I firmly believe education in the arts is both basic and significant in providing young people important skills for the workplace."—*Jim Bennett, Secretary and General Counsel, Maytag Corporation*

Benefit Two: Success in School

Success in society, of course, is predicated on success in school. Any music teacher or parent of a music student can call to mind anecdotes about effectiveness of music study in helping children become better students. Skills learned through the discipline of music, these stories commonly point out, transfer to study skills, communication skills, and cognitive skills useful in every part of the curriculum. Another common variety of story emphasizes the way that the discipline of music study—particularly through participation in ensembles—helps students learn to work effectively in the school environment without resorting to violent or inappropriate behavior. And there are a number of hard facts that we can report about the ways that music study is correlated with success in school:

- Students with coursework/experience in music performance and music appreciation scored higher on the SAT: 53 points higher on the verbal and 39 points higher on the math for music performance, and 61 points higher on the verbal and 42 points higher on the math for music appreciation than students with no arts participation.—*1999 College-Bound Seniors National Report: Profile of SAT Program Test Takers, The College Entrance Examination Board, Princeton, New Jersey*

- Data from the National Education Longitudinal Study of 1988 showed that music participants received more academic honors and awards than non-music students, and that the percentage of music participants receiving As, As/Bs, and Bs was higher than the percentage of non-participants receiving those grades.—*NELS:88 First Follow-up, 1990, National Center for Education Statistics, Washington, DC*
- Physician and biologist Lewis Thomas studied the undergraduate majors of medical school applicants. He found that 66% of music majors who applied to medical school were admitted, the highest percentage of any group. 44% of biochemistry majors were admitted.—*As reported in "The Case for Music in the Schools," Phi Delta Kappan, February 1994*
- A study of 811 high school students indicated that the proportion of minority students with a music teacher role-model was significantly larger than for any other discipline. 36% of these students identified music teachers as their role models, as opposed to 28% English teachers, 11% elementary teachers, 7% physical education/sports teachers, and 1% principals.—*D. L. Hamann and L. M. Walker, "Music teachers as role models for African-American students," Journal of Research in Music Education, 41, 1993*
- Students who participated in arts programs in selected elementary and middle schools in New York City showed significant increases in self-esteem and thinking skills.—*National Arts Education Research Center, New York University, 1990*

Benefit Three: Success in Developing Intelligence

Success in school and in society depends on an array of abilities. Without joining the intense ongoing debate about the nature of intelligence as a basic ability, we can demonstrate that some measures of a child's intelligence are indeed increased with music instruction. Once again, this burgeoning range of data supports a long-established base of anecdotal knowledge to the effect that music education makes kids smarter. What is new and especially compelling, however, is a combination of tightly controlled behavioral studies and groundbreaking neurological research that shows how music study can actively contribute to brain development:

- A research team exploring the link between music and intelligence reported that music training is far superior to computer instruction in dramatically enhancing children's abstract reasoning skills, the skills necessary for learning math and science.—*Shaw, Rauscher, Levine, Wright, Dennis and Newcomb, "Music training causes long-term enhancement of preschool children's spatial-temporal reasoning," Neurological Research, vol. 19, February 1997*

- Students in two Rhode Island elementary schools who were given an enriched, sequential, skill-building music program showed marked improvement in reading and math skills. Students in the enriched program who had started out behind the control group caught up to statistical equality in reading, and pulled ahead in math.—*Gardiner, Fox, Jeffrey and Knowles, as reported in Nature, May 23, 1996*

- Researchers at the University of Montreal used various brain imaging techniques to investigate brain activity during musical tasks and found that sight-reading musical scores and playing music both activate regions in all four of the cortex's lobes; and that parts of the cerebellum are also activated during those tasks.—*J. Sergent, E. Zuck, S. Tenial, and B. MacDonall (1992). Distributed neural network underlying musical sight reading and keyboard performance. Science, 257, 106-109*

- Researchers in Leipzig found that brain scans of musicians showed larger planum temporale (a brain region related to some reading skills) than those of non-musicians. They also found that the musicians had a thicker corpus callosum (the bundle of nerve fibers that connects the two halves of the brain) than those of non-musicians, especially for those who had begun their training before the age of seven.—*G. Schlaug, L. Jancke, Y. Huang, and H. Steinmetz (1994). "In vivo morphometry of interhemispheric assymetry and connectivity in musicians." In I. Deliege (Ed.), Proceedings of the 3d international conference for music perception and cognition (pp. 417–418), Liege, Belgium*

- A University of California (Irvine) study showed that after eight months of keyboard lessons, preschoolers showed a 46% boost in their spatial reasoning IQ.—*Rauscher, Shaw, Levine, Ky and Wright, "Music and Spatial Task Performance: A Causal Relationship," University of California, Irvine, 1994*

- Researchers found that children given piano lessons significantly improved in their spatial- temporal IQ scores (important for some types of mathematical reasoning) compared to children who received computer lessons, casual singing, or no lessons.—*F. H. Rauscher, G. L. Shaw, L. J. Levine, E. L. Wright, W. R. Dennis, and R. Newcomb (1997) Music training causes long-term enhancement of preschool children's spatial temporal reasoning. Neurological Research, 19, 1–8*

- A McGill University study found that pattern recognition and mental representation scores improved significantly for students given piano instruction over a three-year period. They also found that self-esteem and musical skills measures improved for the students given piano instruction.—*E. Costa-Giomi, (1998, April). The McGill Piano Project: Effects of three years of piano instruction on children's cognitive abilities, academic achievement, and self-esteem. Paper presented at the meeting of the Music Educators National Conference, Phoenix, AZ, 1998.*

- Researchers found that lessons on songbells (a standard classroom instrument) led to significant improvement of spatial-temporal scores for three- and four-year-olds.—*J. E. Gromko, and A. S. Poorman (1998), The effect of music training on preschooler's spatial-temporal task performance, Journal of Research in Music Education, 46, 173-181* (see reprint of article in this book)

- In the kindergarten classes of the school district of Kettle Moraine, Wisconsin, children who were given music instruction scored 48 percent higher on spatial-temporal skill tests than those who did not receive music training.—*F. H. Rauscher, and M. A. Zupan, (2000), Classroom keyboard instruction improves kindergarten children's spatial-temporal performance: A field study (In press), Early Childhood Research Quarterly*

- An Auburn University study found significant increases in overall self-concept of at-risk children participating in an arts program that included music, movement, dramatics and art, as measured by the Piers-Harris Children's Self-Concept Scale.—*N. H. Barry, Project ARISE: Meeting the needs of disadvantaged students through the arts, Auburn University, 1992*

Benefit Four: Success in Life

Each of us wants our children—and the children of all those around us—to achieve success in school, success in employment, and success in the social structures through which we move. But we also want our children to experience "success" on a broader scale. Participation in music, often as not based on a grounding in music education during the formative school years, brings countless benefits to each individual throughout life. The benefits may be psychological or spiritual, and they may be physical as well:

- A study conducted at Michigan State University found that group keyboard lessons given to older Americans had the dramatic effect of increasing the human growth hormone by 92%. The study also showed significant decreases in anxiety, depression and loneliness—three factors that are critical in coping with stress, stimulating the immune system and improving health.—*Dr. Frederick Tims, reported in AMC Music News, June 2, 1999 (Major funding for this study was provided by NAMM—the Internation Music Products Association, and The National Academy of Recording Arts & Sciences, Inc.)*

- Music education opens doors that help children pass from school into the world around them—a world of work, culture, intellectual activity, and human involvement. The future of our nation depends on providing our children with a complete education that includes music.—*Gerald Ford, former President, United States of America*

- During the Gulf War, the few opportunities I had for relaxation I always listened to music, and it brought to me great peace of mind. I have shared my love of music with people throughout this world, while listening to the drums and special instruments of the Far East, Middle East, Africa, the Carribbean, and the Far North—and all of this started with the music appreciation course that I was taught in a third-grade elementary class in Princeton, New Jersey. What a tragedy it would be if we lived in a world where music was not taught to children.—*H. Norman Schwarzkopf, General, U.S. Army, retired*

- Music is about communication, creativity, and cooperation, and, by studying music in school, students have the opportunity to build on these skills, enrich their lives, and experience the world from a new perspective.—*Bill Clinton, President of the United States of America*

- The arts enrich communities and employees, and also stimulate the kind of intellectual curiosity our company needs to stay competitive.—*Norman R. Augustine, Chairman and Chief Executive Officer, Martin Marietta Corporation*
- A grounding in the arts will help our children to see; to bring a uniquely human perspective to science and technology. In short, it will help them as they grow smarter to also grow wiser.—*Robert E. Allen, Chairman and Chief Executive Officer, AT&T Corporation, in "America's Culture Begins with Education"*

Education is often seen as a way to shape the future. Music education is an important tool for accomplishing this goal by preparing students for success in society, in school, in developing intelligence, and in life. But music education offers even more.

Music education is one way of connecting with the past. Every human culture uses music as what scholars call a "culture carrier"—or what most of us would call a way of life. And the study of music allows students to connect with this rich heritage. It is, of course, a discipline that calls for effort, concentration, and emotional strength on the part of students. And it is a discipline that calls for support from our social institutions.

But most of all, music is caught up in the present. To watch a child (or an adult) interact with music is to watch an individual focused on a moment's magic as a sound is shaped. And the moment stretches from a single sound to a group of notes, to a phrase, to a complete piece. And that piece of eternity is one that comes from the individual. Sometimes it is one that comes from cooperation with other musicians in an ensemble. It often receives contributions from the members of an audience. And it always builds on a culture. The unique blend of intellectual and physical culture encapsulated in that moment—and the preparation that led to that moment—is unmatched in power.

Ardene Shafer is director of outreach at MENC—The National Association for Music Education. Michael Blakeslee is associate executive director for programs at MENC.

Straight Talk about Music and Brain Research

Ella Wilcox

In this article, researchers and educators offer their observations about music and its impact on development and academic achievement. Many questions remain, but the basic research is showing benefits of music study and supporting its place in the curriculum.

There's a lot of discussion these days in the media about the benefits of music in the lives of people of all ages, especially children. The so-called "Mozart effect" has received considerable worldwide attention, and many claims are made about music's value (or lack thereof) vis-a-vis intelligence, development, academic performance, and personality. What can music educators say with certainty when they discuss the advantages of music study for all children? What can music education actually do for students, and at what ages are the effects most noticeable?

Considerable Research

The good news is that there is considerable research that supports the value of music education. Here are some findings that have been replicated in careful research:

Even before birth, young children are able hear music. According to Dr. Joyce Huffaker, a neonatologist at Kaiser Permanente–Los Angeles, "Clinically, it's apparent that babies respond to sound stimuli by the third trimester" of pregnancy. (Prenatal music, however, should not be loud or aimed directly at the mother's abdomen, cautions Janet diPietro, a developmental psychologist at Johns Hopkins University School of Hygiene and Public Health.) In cultures worldwide, toddlers are taught by simple exposure to sounds to pronounce words in their language with ease. These children can also be taught to appreciate Asian tonal structures or

This chapter is reprinted from Ella Wilcox, "Straight Talk about Music and Brain Research," *Teaching Music* 7, no. 3 (December 1999). Copyright 1999 by MENC.

Corelli sonatas, and it will be much easier (and more enjoyable) to understand such music and many other subjects later in life if the young child has built a basic "sound bank" on which to draw.

Wendy Sims, a professor of music education at the University of Missouri–Columbia and chair of MENC's Society for Research in Music Education, states, "Researchers have found that, during the preschool and primary years, children demonstrate very positive attitudes toward many kinds of music. This is an ideal time to capitalize on their open, accepting responses and introduce them to music from a wide range of genres, styles, and cultures." Sims adds, "Using nonverbal assessment methods, investigators have found that children are able to perceive and respond to many more sophisticated musical discriminations than their limited vocabulary allows them to express. Young children need to be provided with stimulating, appropriate experiences and opportunities to create a strong foundation on which future music learning can be built."

Moving to music, dancing, playing instruments, and experimentation with materials that make sounds are all helpful to the development of toddlers. It is the doing, in addition to the listening, that offers the greatest positive benefit in all aspects of learning, especially in music. Studies that reveal significant changes in children's spatial and cognitive development almost all involve the child as actor, not spectator. This is also true of preschoolers through mid-elementary children. The more a child participates, the more wonder and learning he or she experiences.

Effects on Young Children

Frances Rauscher of the University of Wisconsin–Oshkosh sometimes feels as though she's opened a Pandora's box when it comes to the music-brain connection. Most of Rauscher's recent work has to do with the effects of music study on young children. However, she says that she and her colleagues also "have found short-term improvement of college students' performance of spatial-temporal tasks after the students listened to a Mozart sonata," findings that "have been replicated by at least three independent laboratories other than our own," although this later work has not yet been published.

Nevertheless, Rauscher adds, "I do still believe that the strongest effects will be found from music instruction. Music instruction appears to have long-lasting benefits for children's spatial-temporal skills, skills that are needed for understanding proportions and ratios. I've replicated this finding, which we originally published in *Neurological Research* in 1997, in two separate school districts in Wisconsin and also in a two-year study with Wisconsin Head Start preschools. A further longitudinal study, which we are preparing to submit for publication, reveals that one year of instruction is not enough to induce long-term benefits, but continued instruction provides continued positive effects. We don't yet know how long is long enough, nor what age is optimal for beginning lessons (although for neurological reasons we believe that younger is better)."

It is, in fact, the results of short-term exposures that seem to be the main subject of controversy. "Studies in which music (or a musical treatment) was provided as a controlled condition showed an improvement in specific spatial abilities in rats and humans," says Eugenia Costa-Giomi of McGill University. She also notes that "other studies failed to find such improvements. In most investigations, the musical intervention ranged from short listening sessions to seven months of music instruction."

Costa-Giomi's latest work, published in the Fall 1999 issue of the *Journal of Research in Music Education,* reveals that children who received individual piano lessons over a period of three years, from the fourth through the sixth grades, made gains over a control group during the first two years of study in the areas of general and spatial cognitive development. At the end of the third year, however, this advantage had disappeared. She suggests that the temporary improvement in general and spatial cognitive abilities "might be of interest to educators searching for ways to help children develop their capabilities," but states that we "should be cautious about setting unrealistic expectations regarding the cognitive benefits of music education."

Music Study

Harry E. Price, a professor and chair of music education at the University of Alabama, says, "Although published studies have been unable to replicate the so-called 'Mozart effect,' some known benefits of music do come into play in the context of music study. Music is powerful and affects human beings at all stages of life, from premature infants to the very elderly." Price, who is also the editor of the *Journal of Research in Music Education,* recently spoke at the 1999 annual meeting of the

National Association of Schools of Music, where he told his audience that musicians seem to have differently structured brains than do non-musicians.

Brain imagery has shown increases in parts of the cerebral hemisphere and in the thickness of neural fibers connecting the two sides of the brain in children who begin stringed-instrument or keyboard study before the age of seven compared to children who are not exposed to this kind of learning. Some scientists theorize that young keyboard and string players are using both hands in ways that twentieth-century American children usually don't have to do.

Price notes that research shows that other parts of the brain come into play as well. Musicians' brains, as they grow, seem well equipped to process new patterns. Other studies, some done as early as 1971, show that musicians seem to have enhanced control over their brain waves, much as do athletes and artists. Results of many studies reveal that musicians generally have higher spatial test scores in adolescence and adulthood than do nonmusicians. "Music study over an extended period, especially starting in the early years," concludes Price, "changes the brain, as may stimulation from any discipline studied from a young age. We don't yet know what all these physical changes mean or how they might lead to improved brain function, but we do know that improved connectivity in the brain's structure may have lifelong implications that can affect everything from learning ability at all ages to memory in the very old. It seems the changes are all for the better."

What happens when children are exposed to a full, balanced, sequential music education? Martha Shackford, a McLean, Virginia, Suzuki educator, has devoted many years to the education of young children all across the United States as well as in several other countries. She states unequivocally, "Children who receive early music study generally are different from the average child. Regardless of natural gifts, native intelligence, or family economics, most children who study music deeply eventually become more confident, more sensitive individuals, and they are usually better listeners. Often, they are leaders in other areas, and they almost universally do well in other subjects at school." If Shackford's personal observation is correct, then such qualities as self-esteem, leadership, and high academic performance are learned behaviors, and music, valuable in itself as a subject of study, offers untold additional benefits that should be the birthright of every child, especially those born into less privileged and typically less stimulating environments.

Not all the answers are available yet, but clues are emerging about what music can bring to young people. What researchers have found and what teachers know from their teaching implies that all children, especially those in at-risk categories, attain numerous tangible and intangible benefits from extensive, sequential music study. Music participants, on average, receive more academic honors and higher grades than do students in the general school population. As a group, students at all levels who study music and the other arts do better at standardized tests. Evaluations like the Scholastic Assessment Test show that students achieve increasingly higher SAT scores as they study music and arts over longer periods of time. (This is, of course, a correlation, not necessarily a causal relationship.) And musically engaged students are less likely to cause disciplinary problems than some other students (*Arts, Education and Americans,* 1980).

Building Music Programs

So far, it's clear that listening to high-quality music is good, experimenting with musical sound is better, and studying music long-term is best. How does this affect those who make decisions about education in general and music programs in particular in child-care contexts and schools? According to Joan Schmidt, member of the board of directors for the National School Boards Association, "School board members need to pay close attention to the research on music and the brain because some of it has profound implications for school governance. For one thing, the research will help us target our investments to bring the greatest return in terms of raising student achievement. It will be years before neuroscientists can produce definitive proof of the long-term benefits of music instruction.

Meanwhile, they have clearly demonstrated that piano instruction in the early grades significantly improves the spatial-temporal reasoning of children in the primary grades. And that's reason enough to build a better music program. But even more compelling is the news that disadvantaged children show the same kinds of improvement. Because poverty is closely tied to poor performance in school, school boards continually seek ways to narrow the gap. Music could be the key to accomplishing that."

In June 1991, the U.S. Department of Labor published a report by the Secretary's Commission on Achieving Necessary Skills (SCANS). Business executives and educators who read the report learned that certain skills were especially needed in the future workplace, including thinking skills, the ability to solve problems and understand complex interrelationships, and the capacity to communicate, cooperate, and be creative. These skills can be learned in the music classroom, because working as a team is a part of every ensemble, and creative solutions must be found for problems students face each day.

Music involvement can help adults stay more alert at any age, including the later years. Growing evidence from music therapists and physicians shows that music can also be used to help manage the effects of anxiety and stress in a variety of medical contexts (*Journal of Music Therapy*, Spring 1999). Since music of choice has been documented as an effective component of pain-control therapy, some dentists and doctors offer music to patients on whom they are working (*Journal of Music Therapy*, Winter 1992).

In summary, research findings are supportive of the value of music. Says Schmidt, "The window of opportunity for music advocates may well be here. But in our eagerness to capitalize on the research findings, we must never forget that music in its own right has already earned its place in the core curriculum." Music needs to be part of the education of every child, and its myriad benefits, both intrinsic and extrinsic, will increasingly be revealed as researchers continue to learn more about the human brain. For now, it's clear that music study at any age can increase the quality of life, and those who teach it are handing present and future generations a gift whose value is only beginning to be understood.

Ella Wilcox is an associate editor in the Publications Department of MENC—The National Association for Music Education.

Research Linking Music and Intelligence: Helpful or Harmful to the String Teaching Profession?

Laura Reed Racin

This article summarizes some of the recent research linking music and intelligence. It cautions music teachers to avoid overstating the implications of this research and offers ways in which they can responsibly use the information to support their music classes, especially string classes.

*M*usic education has been enjoying a great deal of publicity concerning research that shows a correlation between music study and improved spatial-temporal reasoning or improved test scores. This so-called neuromusicology research—a term coined by *New York Times* critic Alex Ross—has been especially welcomed by the string teaching community and is often used to advocate for new string programs, as well as for additional funding for existing programs.[1]

But some leaders of the music education profession warn that the publicity could backfire, and that advocating for music programs because it aids learning in other areas could be detrimental to the long-term future of music programs in schools. While many teachers in the field are rejoicing over the positive publicity music education is receiving, many scholars and philosophers are concerned about potential negative effects of the media hype.

This chapter is reprinted from Laura Reed Racin, "Research Linking Music and Intelligence: Helpful or Harmful to the String Teaching Profession?" *American String Teacher* 49, no. 1 (February 1999). Copyright 1999 by American String Teacher Association with National School Orchestra Association. Used by permission.

The Research: A Summary

The sidebar (on pages 22 and 23) titled "Music as a Window into Higher Brain Function—Research Chronology" summarizes several studies relating music education and the brain. The information was provided by the American Music Conference (AMC), an advocacy arm of the National Association of Music Merchants.

MENC: The National Association for Music Education regularly publishes statistics linking SAT performance with experience in music. "Students with music course work or experience tend to score thirty-seven to sixty-two points higher than students with no course work or experience in music, based on 1997 results."[2] The most up-to-date statistics from Educational Testing Service can be found on the MENC web site at http://www.menc.org.

Two other recent research studies were summarized in an April 22, 1998, Reuters News Service story: "Neuroscientist Christo Pantev and colleagues at the University of Muenster in Germany...discovered that the musicians' auditory cortex, which responds to pitching a sound on a piano, was about 25 percent larger than their non-musical counterparts. The researchers also found that the younger the musicians began their training, the more the cortex developed.

"The study, reported in the scientific journal *Nature,* supports earlier research that showed a difference in the part of the brain controlling the left and right hand fingers of string musicians," the report continued. "We found that the representation of the fingers of the left hand are bigger than the representation of the fingers of the right hand,' Pantev said."[3]

Maggie Fox filed a story with Reuters on May 22, 1996, that described a study by Martin Gardiner, who tested school children between ages five and seven. "Half got an extra hour of music and visual arts training while the rest had the standard classroom music and drawing sessions. ...The children who got extra music and art showed a marked improvement in mathematics skills."[4]

A cursory library search on the subject heading "cognitive musicology" revealed additional research conducted in 1997 by Robert Zatorre at McGill University and Diana Deutsch of the University of California in San Diego on the relationship between the ways music and language are represented in the brain.[5] Richard Frackowiak at the Institute of

Neurology in London, England, examined what parts of the brain are activated when a subject listens to music.[6] Several researchers reported findings from studies that examine the regions of the brain activated by music listening and participation at the November 1998 meeting of the Society for Neuroscience in Los Angeles.[7]

In addition to studies published in scientific journals, reports of other neuromusicology research have surfaced. Joyce Eastlund Gromko and Allison Smith Poorman investigated "the effect of music training on preschoolers' Performance IQ"[8] David Merrell wanted to know if the choice of music would affect the performance of mice traveling through a maze and found that the mice who listened to classical music outperformed those who listened to heavy-metal.[9] Wilfried Gruhn wrote about "The Influence of Learning on Cortical Activation Patterns" in the *Bulletin of the Council for Research in Music Education*.[10]

Recent Publicity

The so-called neuromusicology research has received a great deal of news media attention in recent years. In February 1996, *Newsweek* magazine featured an extensive article titled "Your Child's Brain."[11] In this article, the importance of early music education was highlighted, and the idea of promoting early string instruction was addressed. Readers were encouraged to put instruments into the hands of youngsters well before the age of ten.

On Sunday, June 14, 1998, *Parade* magazine featured an article titled "Will Piano Lessons Make My Child Smarter?"[12] In this article, Vadim Prokhorov cited a number of schools that are emphasizing music as part of the core curriculum and provided a list of hints for encouraging children in the area of music from infants through school age. The May 1998 issue of *Parents* magazine featured the article "Raising Smart Kids," which highlighted the importance of music lessons, and Gordon Shaw's study on spatial reasoning was cited.[13]

The book *The Mozart Effect* by Don Campbell has generated a tremendous amount of publicity about links between music and the human brain.[14] Numerous articles and news reports have covered this book, which deals specifically with the potential healing power of music.

The cable channel VH1 has launched a "Save the Music" campaign and presented a concert to raise public awareness about music education. Celine Dion, Aretha Franklin, Gloria Estefan, Shania Twain, and Mariah Carey performed at this event. About the recent research linking music and brain activity, VH1 President John Sykes stated, "Music education is not a luxury. We now have solid proof that early music instruction builds brain power and positively affects basic math and verbal skills."[15]

On August 19, 1998, the television show Dateline NBC featured a story about New York City's public school No. 144, at which piano lessons are given to kindergarten children. In that piece, experts recommended the violin as the optimum instrument for young children and stated that music lessons should begin at age four.

News services, such as the Associated Press and Reuters, provide regular news coverage of the music-and-brain research studies, especially as the studies are to be published in the journals *Science* and *Nature*. Countless daily newspapers and radio stations have picked up the stories filed on these news services.

In the trade press, *Symphony* magazine featured an article titled, "Music's Brain Power."[16] The fall 1997 issue of *The School Music Dealer* featured as its cover story "Music and the Brain: How Recent Studies Linking Music to Learning Can Positively Affect Your Business."[17] Many newsletters published by music dealers, instrument manufacturers, and state or local music educator associations regularly contain articles on the topic of neuromusicology research.

Using the Information in Advocacy Efforts

Some music teachers, and especially string teachers, have found creative ways to use neuromusicology research to advocate the importance of music education. Teachers in Phoenix, Arizona, for example, have developed a set of concert program covers that highlight the positive benefits that participation in music provides for children. Wayne Roederer, string specialist of the Mesa Public Schools, explains, "This reading material meets with a captive audience. We never pass up an opportunity to educate parents as well as students."[18]

The information is often used in public speaking. *The Mozart Effect* author Don Campbell served as the keynote speaker for the Suzuki Association of the America's 1998 national conference in Chicago and as keynote speaker at the opening concert of the St. Louis Symphony's summer season. String teachers have used the information in speaking engagements at meetings of community service organizations, such as Kiwanis and Lions Club.

The American Music Conference has suggested several ways that this information is relevant to string teachers in the sidebar on page 25 titled "Putting the Research to Work for Strings."

Some leading music education scholars and philosophers, however, warn that many problems are involved with using the neuromusicology research to advocate for music education programs. Three main issues are involved in the controversy: questions about the soundness of the research being publicized; problems inherent in communicating scientific research to a mass audience; and basing a philosophy of music education on non-musical benefits of music study.

Soundness of the Research

Richard Colwell, chair of music education at the New England Conservatory, visiting professor of music education at the University of Michigan, and recent inductee into the MENC Hall of Fame, said that he and others "have expressed doubts about much of this research because it has not been subjected to the normal review procedures."[19] The issue is examined by Elliott Eisner in an *Art Education* article and by Colwell and others in a symposium issue of *Arts Education Policy Review,* coordinated by David Pankratz.[20]

Much of the debate concerns randomization of research design. "The fact that students who study the arts for four years in high school have higher SAT scores tells us only that music programs are attracting the better students," Colwell pointed out. "Students who receive string instruction are not the run-of-the-mill student. That is a concern of Rauscher as well. The students she had available were enrolled in a preschool program, and parents who provide this experience are not a random sample of parents."

Nancy Whitaker, professor of music at Northwestern University, also questioned the choice of music used in the studies.[21] "Would people of all cultures have the same response to these musical patterns of expectation?" Whitaker asked. "Other researchers—for example Rideout, Fairchild, and Wernert—have found that other music might work just as well, even the music of Yanni, whose compositions are similar in structure, tempo, melodic and harmonic consonance, and predictability.[22] Wilson and Brown reexamine the Mozart effect thoroughly in *The Journal of Psychology*," Whitaker pointed out.[23]

As Whitaker said, "the music education profession risks getting a bad name in the larger educational and scientific community when we place our eggs in a basket constructed too far from scientific reality." The majority of practicing string teachers in the field may not have the background, time, or desire to decipher research to determine how a study was constructed. Northwestern University Professor Emeritus Bennett Reimer advised, "Readers must be extremely cautious of reported research results, because complexities and uncertainties in the research are often glossed over in order to dramatize the findings."

> ## How the Brain Learns
>
> The November issue of *Educational Leadership,* Vol. 56, No. 3 (November 1998) is a theme issue called "How the Brain Learns." Two articles in this issue are of particular interest to music teachers: "Art for the Brain's Sake," by Robert Sylvester, and "The Music in Our Minds," by Norman W. Weinberger. According to Thomas Regelski, "This issue is probably the most thorough, well-balanced account of brain research in relation to education heretofore available for the general reader. Many school administrators subscribe to this publication, so music teachers can borrow the issue from their own principals and then refer their principals to specific parts that support their own contentions."

Over-Statement of Results

"Those who seek to provide a rationale for music education based on claims for the non-musical contribution of musical study and experience to cognitive functioning cite research that is scattered, non-systematic, and far from scientifically conclusive," Thomas A. Regelski, distinguished professor of music at State University of New York in Fredonia, asserted.[24] "The resulting conclusions and claims for advocacy, unfortunately, are thus far from warranted in any scientific sense, and tend to be very misleading and potentially dangerous if taken literally."

When many pages of scientific research are distilled into a couple of sentences, the fine distinctions within and between each study are lost on most readers. Richard Colwell, editor of MENC's *Handbook of Research* on *Music Teaching and Learning* and founding editor of the *Bulletin of the Council for Research in Music Education,* noted, "Frances Rauscher herself has made the point that a correlation does not mean causation. Just because she and Gordon Shaw have found rather high correlations between music and spatial-temporal reasoning does not mean that music *causes* an increase in this kind of reasoning." When science meets the popular press the result is often an over-statement and over-generalization of research findings.

By providing concise summaries of the studies in laymen's terms, the AMC hopes to provide string teachers with ammunition to improve advocacy efforts. String teachers are generally thankful to receive a summary of the research; practicing teachers, for the most part, do not have

---

Music as a Window into Higher Brain Function— Research Chronology

The following information was released by the American Music Conference. It is intended to assist journalists in reporting about the benefits of music education. It is also intended as a set of "talking points" for public speakers and others advocating for music education. The information is reprinted here verbatim from the AMC document.

1985 Gordon Shaw, Dennis Silverman, and John Pearson present the trion model of the brain's neuronal structure. (Proceedings of the National Academy of Sciences. USA 82 [1985]: 2364–2368).

1989 Experiments in which musicians perform mental rehearsals of music indicate that music and other creative skills, such as mathematics and chess, may involve extremely precise firing patterns by billions of brain neurons. (Leslie Brothers and Gordon Shaw, *Models of Brain Function,* edited by R. Cotterill. Cambridge: Cambridge University Press, 1989).

1990 Computer experiments reveal that trion firing patterns can be mapped onto pitches and instrument timbres to produce music. This suggests that the trion model is a viable model for the coding of certain aspects of musical structure in human composition and perception, and that the trion model is relevant for examining creativity in higher cognitive functions, such as mathematics and chess, that are similar to music. (Xiaodan Leng, Gordon Shaw, and Eric Wright, *Music Perception,* Vol. 8, No. 1 [Fall 1990]: 49–62).

1991 Xiaodan Leng and Gordon Shaw propose that music may be considered a "pre-language," and that early music training may be useful in "exercising" the brain for certain higher cognitive functions. (*Concepts in Neuroscience,* Vol. 2, No. 2 [1991]: 29–258).

the time to decipher pages and pages of scientific research. The teacher, however, has a responsibility to avoid overstating the results of the studies. Precise language is needed when trying to communicate information to parents, school boards, and other members of local communities. Terms such as *significant, proves* or *confirms, causal effects,* and *cognitive functioning* have very different meanings to the scientific community than to the lay community.

Advocacy vs. Philosophy

At the MENC national conference in Phoenix, April 1998, Frances Rauscher herself said at a well-attended session, "It's a shame that music

---

Music as a Window into Higher Brain Function— Research Chronology—cont.

1993 Pilot study finds that preschool children given music training display significant improvement in spatial reasoning ability. Experiments with college students find that, after listening to a Mozart sonata, they experience a significant although temporary gain in spatial reasoning skills.

1994 Stage II follow-up to pilot study again finds that music training improves spatial reasoning in preschool children. This gain does not occur in those without music training. (Frances Rauscher, Gordon Shaw, Linda Levine, and Katherine Ky, paper presented at the American Psychological Association, Los Angeles, [August 1994]).

1995 Followup to first Mozart study confirms that listening to Mozart improves spatial reasoning, and that this effect can increase with repeated testing over days. However, the effect may not occur when music lacks sufficient complexity. (Frances Rauscher, Gordon Shaw, and Katherine Ky, *Neuroscience Letters,* Vol. 185 [1995]: 44–47).

1997 Stage III of Drs. Shaw and Rauscher's research suggests preschoolers who receive music training—particularly keyboard lessons—show significant improvements in their spatial-temporal reasoning skills above those in their peer group who receive computer training or no training. (Gordon Shaw, Frances Rauscher, Linda Levine, Eric Wright, Wendy Dennis, and Robert Newcomb, *Neurological Research,* Vol. 19 [February 1997]).

---

education would have to be justified on the basis of the research I do." The audience applauded enthusiastically. Of the incident Bennett Reimer observed, "Fifty years ago her statement wouldn't have received a positive response, but today we better understand the intrinsic value of music and have adopted a philosophy of music based on the aesthetic value of music. It's almost insulting to the profession of music education to have to justify programs based on the fact that music study aids learning in other areas or has extra-musical benefits. It is a terrible way to justify music education."

"Even if the research and related claims were true, the claimed benefits would be unremarkable in providing the sought-for rationale for music education, because just about any complex mental, perceptual or psychomotor activity, practice or study at an early age can be expected to produce certain changes in neural and thus cognitive development," Thomas Regelski pointed out. "Any rationale predicated on the purported contribution of music to the improved development of general intelligence, intellect, reasoning, and learning also falls prey to a variety of serious problems."

"The argument of the relationship between math and music has never been very convincing," Richard Colwell added. "Music educators were concerned that if our objective was to improve math outcomes then it just might be that teaching more math would be more effective than more music. The teachers of Latin used the argument that the study of Latin improved the study of English until some clever chap suggested that taking more English might be a better solution to deficiencies in English education."

"Basing a rationale on purported non-musical benefits reduces the value of music instruction to a secondary role as hand maiden to teaching other subjects," Regelski explained. "Advocating music on claims for general brain and cognitive development—even if they were indisputable, which they are not—thus diminishes the value of music to the lowly status of a means to other, seemingly more important non-musical ends. The value of music in its own right is thereby denied in the minds of students, parents, and taxpayers."

Sally Utley of Columbia, South Carolina posed the following request via "Fun Music Ideas," an email-delivered newsletter: "My principal called yesterday. She had been to a workshop that said math scores could be raised by using music. She would like me to teach 'music math' to

Putting the Research to Work

The American Music Conference provided the following suggestions of how recent neuromusicology research might be used to advocate for more and bigger string programs.

- Bring news articles on the subject to the attention of administrators and curriculum developers in a proactive manner, when times are good. Too often, this information is only used for damage control when programs are in jeopardy.
- Educate colleagues as to the benefits of music and string instruction. Many string teachers must pull students out of classes in order to provide instruction, at times to the chagrin of classroom teachers. The media coverage of current research can serve as a catalyst to positive discussion among teachers.
- Make administrators and the community aware of the benefits to beginning music instruction at an early age and that stringed instruments can be played by very young students because smaller sized instruments are available and pedagogically viable. Administrators may be more willing to consider string instruction beginning at earlier grade levels.
- Make information available to parents of students enrolled in a school string program to make retention easier to deal with at the middle and high school levels.
- Use the research to encourage high school students to consider string education as a career. Joanne Erwin, associate professor of music education at Oberlin Conservatory, pointed out that "Many prospective teachers incorrectly think that teaching elementary music would be boring because the music is relatively basic. The current research simply reinforces the impact that music teachers can have on a child's development." She adds, "This research and publicity also may help more performing musicians realize the importance of teaching music to young people."

third and fourth graders in addition to my regular music classes. Does anyone have any possible resources for a class such as this?" Although Utley is happy to teach "music math," because it is an addition to her duties as a music teacher, her situation shows the potential effects of the neuromusicology research.

"In all the research, nowhere do we read what the role of music educators should be in helping to develop cognitive functioning," Reimer said. "The research doesn't tell music educators what, how, or when music education is supposed to accomplish the stated results. Nowhere does this research suggest any kind of curriculum or what we are supposed to be doing to improve spatial reasoning. In many ways, we are arguing ourselves out of a job because there is no inherent curriculum in the rationale that music study improves spatial reasoning.

"The research raises many issues of accountability," Reimer continued. "If we claim we can improve spatial temporal ability, then we are going to be held accountable for proving that we can do so. We would have to completely change our teaching to achieve these results. Many other activities could develop spatial reasoning better than music education, so if this is our reason for being, then we really aren't needed at all."

"Instead of advocacy based on weak and misleading claims, a rationale for music education must be firmly grounded in a philosophy of music—what music is and is good for in making a life worth living—focusing on the distinctive contribution music can make to the individual's general education," Regelski offered. Many such philosophies of music education have been put forth in recent years. Regelski has published articles on his praxial theory of music and music education in the *Canadian Music Educator* (Spring 1997) and *Philosophy of Music Education Review* (Spring 1998). David Elliott has also received recent attention for the ideas put forth in his book *Music Matters: A New Philosophy of Music Education* (Oxford University Press, 1994). Bennett Reimer is well-known for his aesthetic philosophies of music education spelled out in the book *A Philosophy of Music Education* (Prentice Hall, 1989).

"We want and need a basis for a curriculum of music education in the schools," Reimer said. "The research cited does not provide such a basis. The National Standards provide the basis for a curriculum of musical learnings—learnings for which music education is essential. These learnings focus on what is uniquely valuable about music—that it provides experiences and satisfactions nothing else can provide."

"The strongest argument for supporting music programs has been the power of music to communicate man's deepest feelings, to use the symbols of music where words fail us," Richard Colwell said.

Helpful or Harmful?

Do the cautions of leading music education scholars and researchers mean that string teachers should have no use for neuromusicology research and the publicity it is generating? Not necessarily.

Despite the potential negative effects of using the research to advocate for music programs, string teachers often find that parents, legislators, and other community leaders respond positively to the argument that music study will aid learning in other areas. Especially in low-income areas, parents who are just trying to survive will probably not be convinced to invest in an instrument or lessons for their children because it adds aesthetic value to life. A string teacher trying to save a school program from the chopping block is going to pull out any and all ammunition to save that program.

"Sometimes we have to say things that people understand and are interested in hearing," Bennett Reimer said. "If improved learning of other things pushes the right buttons, them I'm all for discussing the additional benefits of music study. I don't mind advocating for music education by saying there seem to be other good effects besides the intrinsic aesthetic value of music study. But we must be careful not to lose sight of the true purpose of music education; non-musical values must be presented as a welcome bonus."

"There is an important difference between a philosophy of music education and advocacy efforts, and *AST* readers need to be clear on that difference," said Robert Gillespie, chair of the String Education Department at Ohio State University. "String teachers should stay abreast of the research and be able to articulate what it *really* means to parents and administrators. Educators should approach the research with caution, be careful not to overstate or over-generalize the results, and use precise language when discussing the studies. But mostly, string teachers can use the publicity surrounding the research as an opportunity to bring up all of the intrinsic reasons for learning to play a stringed instrument."

References

1. Alex Ross, "Listening to Prozac ... Er, Mozart." *New York Times* August 28, 1994, H23.

2. "News Shorts," *Teaching Music* 5 (February 1998): 13.

3. Reuters News Service, April 22, 1998.

4. Reuters News Service, London, May 22, 1996.

5. "In One Ear and Out the Other," *The Economist* 342 (February 22, 1997): 90–91.

6. Josie Glausiusz, "The Neural Orchestra," *Discover* 18 (September

1997): 28.

7. Robert Lee Hotz, "The Power of Music," *Los Angeles Times* November 11, 1998.

8. Joyce Eastlund Gromko and Allison Smith Poorman, "The Effect of Music Training on Preschoolers' Spatial-Temporal Task Performance," *Journal of Research in Music Education* 46 (Summer 1998): 173–81.

9. Vadim Prokhorov, "Will Piano Lessons Make My Child Smarter?" *Parade* Magazine, June 14, 1998, 14–17.

10. Wilfried Gruhn, "The Influence of Learning on Cortical Activation Patterns," *Bulletin of the Council for Research in Music Education* 133 (Summer 1997): 25–30.

11. Sharon Begley, "Your Child's Brain," *Newsweek* 127 (February 19, 1996): 54–8+.

12. Vadim Prokhorov, "Will Piano Lessons Make My Child Smarter?" *Parade* Magazine, June 14, 1998, 14–17.

13. Laurel Graeber, "Raising Smart Kids," *Parents* 73 (May 1998): 134–6.

14. Don Campbell. *The Mozart Effect* (New York: Avon Books, 1997).

15. From "Music/Arts Education Quotable Quotes," media kit document, American Music Conference. 1998.

16. John Mahlmann, "Music's Brain Power: Tapping In," *Symphony* 47 (Sept./Oct. 1996): 18–24, 54.

17. Romina Shane, "Music and the Brain," *School Music Dealer* (Fall 1997), 18–22, 36–37.

18. Phone interview with Scott Laird.

19. Correspondence from Richard Colwell to Laura Racin, July 31, 1998.

20. Elliot Eisner, "Does Experience in the Arts Boost Academic Achievement?" *Art Education* 51 (January 1998): 7–16; David Pankratz, "A Long Trail Awinding: Issues, Interests, and Priorities in Arts Education Research," *Arts Education Policy Review* 99 (May/June 1998): 21–29.

21. Correspondence from Nancy Whitaker to Laura Racin, August 15, 1998.

22. B. Rideout, R. Fairchild, and L. Wernert, "The Effect of Music on Spatial Performance: A Test of Generality," Presented at the Eastern Psychological Association, Washington, DC, 1997.

23. T. Wilson and T. Brown, "Reexamination of the Effect of Mozart's Music on Spatial-Task Performance," *The Journal of Psychology,* 131 (no. 4 1997): 365–370.

24. Correspondence from Thomas Regelski to Laura Racin, August 8, 1998.

Laura Reed Racin is editor of American String Teacher *and a string instructor for the Fairmont State Community College Music Program in West Virginia.*

Music and
Young Children

Lessons of the Music Womb

Norman M. Weinberger

Young children and even infants are known to have surprisingly complex abilities to perceive and respond to basic components of music. This musical competency, evident long before the development of speech or the ability to play a musical instrument, raises the question of the earliest age at which the nervous system and brain can adequately process, learn, and remember music. Increasing evidence suggests that the answer is "well before birth." In short, the womb appears to be the first concert hall.

Toward the latter part of the 19th Century there arose, as never before, a great interest in understanding the mental capabilities of animals. Energized by Darwin's writings, both scientists and the lay public became fascinated with the animal mind. Anecdotes were gathered and published, usually attesting to an animal's remarkable, one might say unbelievable, powers. One such report concerned two mice in the countryside who found themselves unable to cross a wide stream. They searched about and, finding a dried cow pie, hauled it to the water's edge. Shoving it into the stream, one got in front and paddled while the other sat at the "stern," using its tail to steer safely to the other side, where they disembarked happy and dry. The truth of this tale was "attested" by the fact that the observer was a local clergyman, whose veracity could hardly be denied. However, he did admit to sipping wine during a picnic with his lady friend while they observed the remarkable intelligence of the two field mice.[1]

It is true that the capabilities of animals have been underestimated. But overestimation is not the appropriate remedy. The corrective is to perform objective and replicable observations of behavior.

Interestingly, the human infant has suffered from the same sort of underestimation as that of animals prior to Darwin's time. In fact, the failure to appreciate the mental capabilities of infants lasted well past the middle of the twentieth century. Because they lack speech and spend so much time eating and sleeping, the presumption was that not much cognition was going on inside the infant head. That view has been largely dissipated with the increasing application of objective, replicable measurement of infant behavior, particularly within the last quarter of the century. One type of competence, previously discussed in these pages (see "The Musical Infant," *MRN*, 1994, I (1), Spring 1994), concerns the fact that infants have considerable musical abilities. For example, they perceive and remember melodic contour, the pattern of rising and falling pitches in a composition. They also recognize a melody as the same when it is played at very different tempi and can instantly notice changes in rhythm that would distort a composition. For all of these basic aspects of music, infant perception and cognition are generally similar to the ways in which adult listeners process music.

Asking about the Developmental Origins of Music

The discovery of musical abilities in infants raises the question of their time of origin. At what age do these types of abilities first appear? This query is related to the long-standing issue of whether infants remember their birth or even their *in utero* experiences. In seeking answers, one finds reports that seem no more credible than the story of the mice and their navigational use of dried cow pies. For example, there are collections of anecdotes which claim that people have detailed memories of birth or even *in utero* experiences. The reliability of these stories has been claimed on the basis either of hypnosis or that similar accounts of the birth are given by parents and children, although the parents claim never to have given children details of their birth. A little girl remembered that her parents argued about her name in the delivery room.[2] A little boy delivered by Caesarian section recalled that it was "funny" when the wall of the uterus opened and the light came in.[3] If these stories are true, then the newborn is able to understand strained social interactions and the detailed nature of conversations at birth and it also has a fine sense of humor. But as such high level cognitive abilities require months or years of development, these stories smell a bit like the cow pies appropriated by the mice for their cruise. Memories of early childhood are notoriously unreliable. That one can be absolutely certain about an early experience but be absolutely wrong about it is well-established.[4]

So if we cannot rely upon personal recollections and anecdotal stories, how is it possible to know whether or not the newborn child, or the fetus in particular, has musical competencies? How can we try to find the beginnings of music?

We have to answer four questions, objectively. First, after conception how long does it take until the fetus can actually hear? Second, do musical sounds from the outside world reach the ears of the fetus? Third, what are the *in utero* responses to sound, particularly music. Fourth, what are the postnatal effects of *in utero* musical stimulation?

Prenatal Behavior

Regarding the beginning of hearing, the ear starts to develop only a few weeks after conception. However, the auditory system of the brain really doesn't function well, if at all, before about the 26th week, that is at the beginning of the last trimester of pregnancy.[5] As to the second question, sound does reach the *in utero* ear, but it is greatly distorted because liquid and tissue surround the fetus. There is relatively little effect on sounds below about middle C on the piano, but an increasing reduction in sound levels with higher notes. As most instruments have harmonics about this frequency, there is a change in timbre. Those instruments having mainly high notes are affected most, such as the trumpet. On the other hand, melody and rhythm are not much altered. In fact, *in utero* recordings of Beethoven's Fifth Symphony yielded a clearly identifiable sound image.[6] Thus, while sounds are greatly altered as they pass from the outside world to the ear of the fetus, there is more than sufficient musical stimulation to be heard in the womb.

What are the responses to music before birth? They consist mainly of body movements and changes in heart rate. Most sounds cause a short-lasting slowing of heart rate, as part of a "What is it?" response. Very loud sounds produce increases in heart rate, often with a startle response.[7] Not only do sounds produce movement and changes in heart rate, but also there is evidence of pre-natal learning. Perhaps the simplest form of learning is habituation, which is learning to stop paying attention to repeated sounds that become boring. If a novel stimulus is substituted, infants will respond to it, showing they noticed the change. During the last trimester of pregnancy, the fetus is clearly capable of habituating to a repeated stimulus applied to the mother's abdomen, and also responding again when the stimulus is changed.[8]

More complex learning can also occur before birth. In one study, the abdomen received a gentle vibratory stimulus that did not itself produce fetal responses; this was followed by a loud sound that did provoke movement. After several paired presentations, the subjects responded to the gentle vibration, showing that they anticipated receiving the loud sound.[9] That this basic type of association can be learned before birth suggests considerable capacity of the fetus to acquire information and remember events.

From Womb to Room

This brings us to the fourth question, the postnatal effects of prenatal music. While one cannot determine all of the effects of prenatal music on the fetus, because of the very limited measures of behavior, the assessment of behavior after birth does allow us to draw conclusions about prenatal effects. Two types of postnatal assessments have been made: the rate of behavioral development and the degree of prenatal learning as measured by postnatal memory.

Some studies suggest that prenatal exposure to music facilitates infant development, and thus might one day serve to alleviate or remediate certain developmental delays in some children. Panthuraampthorn and his colleagues enlisted expectant mothers in a stimulation regimen that included music, rocking and patting the abdomen from 28–36 weeks of gestational age.[10] They stated that large proportions of infants showed early development of the ability to orient toward their mother's voice. However the role of music itself is unclear because of the use of other stimuli and the findings themselves may not be significant due to the lack of a control comparison group. However Blum used a prenatal program (Leonardo 180) consisting of various types of music. He reported facilitated development in orienting to sound, babbling, visual tracking and motor control.[11] Although there was no control group lacking music, the author did show that the behaviors exceeded population norms.

LaFuente did include a control group in her study of the effects of music on the rate of postnatal development.[12] Beginning the 28th to 30th weeks, mothers played tapes of basic elements of music, progressing over weeks from a three note major chord through more complex chords, for a total of 50 to 90 hours across subjects. During infancy the music group exhibited significantly more rapid development of many behaviors, including babbling, visual tracking, eye-hand coordination, exploring objects with the mouth, facial imitation, general motor coordination and ability to hold the bottle with both hands.

All of these findings are mutually consistent and certainly point to the potential importance of prenatal music on development. However it must be realized that the results consist mainly of the mothers' judgments and therefore unconscious bias cannot be absolutely ruled out. Future studies in which a neutral researcher, who does not know whether a child was in the experimental or control group, would solve this problem.

Last, we take up the issue of whether there is prenatal learning of music. Although few studies have been performed, they agree not only that music can be learned *in utero* but that it can also be remembered after birth. For example, one study reported that one-week-old infants prefer the lullaby sung by their mothers during pregnancy. Another investigation found that the prenatal lullaby had a greater soothing effect than a control song. There is also a report that maternal involvement in a prenatal music program increases bonding between mothers and their infants, although the basis for this effect is presently obscure.[13]

In a related but more extensive investigation, Peter Hepper of Queen's University, Belfast, Northern Ireland, studied prenatal and postnatal responses to music, specifically the theme tunes of popular television shows viewed by their mothers.[14] It was estimated that the mothers in the TV group watched a show, the "Neighbors," 360 times during pregnancy. When tested 2 to 4 days after birth, the music group of infants showed a significant decrease in heart rate to the theme song from the show compared to a control group. To determine if the music learning was highly specific, a follow-up experiment used a different piece of music to which the mothers and fetuses had never been exposed. The neonates did not respond to this song. Moreover, another group exhibited no responses to the song played backwards. Both results demonstrate that fetal learning of and memory for music are extremely specific.

To determine the gestational age of learning, Hepper first studied fetuses near term, 36 to 37 weeks of age. Repeated exposure to the selected piece of music resulted in subsequent *in utero* movement responses to that composition, compared to controls. However, no such learning could be found in fetuses of 29 to 30 weeks gestational age. Here then, we have very direct evidence of the origin of prenatal musical learning.

Recall that the auditory system starts to be functional at about week 26. Thus, it seems clear that the ability to learn and remember music requires much additional development, at least beyond week 30.

In conclusion, study of the developmental origins of human mental and behavioral capabilities and the prenatal environment within which they emerge is growing rapidly. This essay concerns music only. Systematic and objective investigations point increasingly to an important role for music in human prenatal development. As with all emerging areas of investigation, these initial studies can only hint at the wealth of information yet to be uncovered. Similarly, the overall implications of the unexpectedly early origins of musical competence can only be dimly glimpsed at this early stage of inquiry. But among these are reappraisals of human nature, grandiose as that may seem. We do need to fully know ourselves, but we don't yet.

Notes

1. Romanes, G.J. (1885). *Animal Intelligence.* New York: Appleton, pg. 364.

2. Chamberlain, D.B. (1988). The mind of the newborn: Increasing evidence of competence. In: *Prenatal and Perinatal Psychology and Medicine,* Fedor-Freybergh, P., and Vogel, M.L.V. Parthenon Publishing, Park Ridge, NJ, pp. 5–22.

3. Laibow, R.E. (1986). Birth recall: A clinical report. *Pre- and Peri-Natal Psychology,* 1:78–81.

4. DuBreuil, S.C., Garry, M., & Loftus, E.F. (1998). Tales from the crib: Age regression and the creation of unlikely memories. In: *Truth in memory.* S.J. Lynn, K.M. McConkey, et al. (Eds.), The Guilford Press, New York, NY, pp. 137–160. Loftus, E.F. (1997). Memories for a past that never was. *Current Directions in Psychological Science,* 6: 60–65.

5. Starr, A., Amlie, R.N., & Martin, W.H., et al. (1977). Development of auditory function in newborn infants revealed by auditory brainstem potentials. *Pediatrics,* 30: 831–839. Werner, L.A. & Marean, G.C. (1996). *Human Auditory Development.* Westview Press, Boulder, CO.

6. Abrams, R.M., Griffiths, K., & Huang, X., et al. (1998). Fetal music perception: The role of sound transmission. *Music Perception,* 15: 307–317.

7. Lecanuet, J.P., Granier-Deferre, C., & Busnel, M.C. (1988). Fetal cardiac and motor responses to octave-band noises as a function of cerebral frequency, intensity and heart rate variability. *Early Human Development,* 18: 81–93.

8. Leader, L.R., Baillie, P., & Martin, B., et al. (1982). The assessment and

significance of habituation to a repeated stimulus by the human fetus. *Early Human Development,* 7: 211–219.

9. Spelt, David K. (1948). The conditioning of the human fetus in utero. *Journal of Experimental Psychology.* 38: 338–347.

10. Panthuraamphorn, C., Dookchitra, D., & Sanmaneechai, M. (1998). The outcome of fetal response and learning to prenatal stimuli. Unpublished manuscript. (I am indebted to Dr. Panthuraamphorn for making available his unpublished paper.)

11. Blum, T. (1998). Human proto-development: Very early auditory stimulation. *International Journal Prenatal and Perinatal Psychology and Medicine,* 10: 447–466.

12. LaFuente, M.J., Grifol, R., & Segarra, J., et al. (1997). Effects of the Firstart method of prenatal stimulation on psychomotor development: The first six months. *Pre and Perinatal Psychology Journal,* 11: 151–162. (Group differences in breast feeding have not been ruled out as contributory).

13. Satt, B.J. (1984). An investigation into the acoustical induction of intrauterine learning. *Dissertation Abstracts,* unpublished doctoral dissertation, California School of Professional Psychology. Polverini-Rey, R.A. (1993). Intraterine musical learning: The soothing effect on newborns of a lullaby learned prenatally. *Dissertation Abstracts,* unpublished doctoral dissertation, California School of Professional Psychology. Shaw, D. (1991). Intrauterine musical learning: A study of its effects on mother-infant bonding. *Dissertation Abstracts,* unpublished doctoral dissertation, California School of Professional Psychology.

One must exercise some caution in the interpretation of studies for which all of the details are not known. This is the case with the three unpublished dissertations listed above. The original and complete doctoral theses were unavailable at the time of writing.

14. Hepper, P. G. (1991). An examination of fetal learning before and after birth, *The Irish Journal of Psychology,* 12: 95–07.

Norman S. Weinberger is professor and director of MuSICA at the Center for the Neurobiology of Learning and Memory in the Department of Neurobiology and Behavior at the University of California at Irvine.

Recent Brain Research on Young Children

John W. Flohr, Daniel C. Miller, and Diane C. Persellin

With the use of technologies such as EEGs (electroencephalograms), researchers can observe and measure the brain activity of young children as they engage in musical tasks and other activities. A recent study has shown that children who received music instruction (which included singing, playing instruments, moving, listening, creating, and prereading/writing activities) showed less brain activity when later completing a visual-spatial task than did students receiving no music instruction. This suggests that the brain processing of the children receiving music instruction was more efficient.

A variety of new research techniques are now being used to investigate brain functioning and development in young children. Preliminary results indicate that music may have an impact on brain activity, especially during the early childhood years, when human development hinges on the interplay between nature and nurture. This article provides information about current research and offers some recommendations for music educators based on recent findings.

Brain Activity

How is music processed in the brains of young children? Intrigued by this question, J. W. Flohr and D. C. Miller used an electroencephalogram (EEG) in 1993 to investigate subtle changes in brain electrical activity ("Quantitative EEG Differences between Baseline and Psychomotor Response to Music," *Music Education Research Reports*, 1993, Texas Music Educators Association). Five-year-old children listened to music by Vivaldi and an Irish folk song while their brain activity was assessed. To focus the children's attention on the music, the researchers

---

This chapter is reprinted from John W. Flohr, Daniel C. Miller, and Diane C. Persellin, "Recent Brain Research on Young Children," *Teaching Music* 6, no. 6 (June 1999). Copyright 1999 by MENC.

asked them to tap a steady beat using rhythm sticks. Increased activity in the temporal regions (auditory centers) of their brains was observed. This finding served to establish the EEG technique as useful with young children and determined that EEG could help localize the brain's response to music. (See the sidebar for information on EEG and other techniques.)

The children were retested two years later, using identical methods (J. W. Flohr and D. C. Miller, "Developmental Quantitative EEG Differences during Psychomotor Response to Music," paper presented at Texas Music Educators Convention, San Antonio, 1995; ERIC Document PS025653). At age five, their responses to the two different styles of music did not produce different EEG readings. At age seven, however, the EEG readings differed depending upon the style of music, particularly in the left temporal region of the brain. The findings suggested that children's brains respond differently to different types of music after the age of five and that these differences can be localized using the EEG technique.

In 1994 and again in 1997, Frances Rauscher and her colleagues used behavioral tests to examine the effect of music instruction on young children's brain functioning. Results of the first study were presented in a paper at the American Psychological Association 102nd Annual Convention, "Music and Spatial Task Performance: A Causal Relationship," in Los Angeles in 1994. Their 1997 study was reported in "Music Training Causes Long Term Enhancement of Preschool Children's Spatial-Temporal Reasoning," *Neurological Research,* vol. 19. They found that children who had received music instruction (including keyboard lessons) scored higher in spatial task ability than those who had not.

The Rauscher study generated much discussion in the music education profession. Concerns arose regarding the publicity generated from this research, the need to replicate it with other groups, and the behavioral testing instruments used. The popular press quickly jumped on the bandwagon, vigorously promoting the positive effects of music instruction, and several articles appeared in popular journals and newspapers such as *Newsweek* (S. Begley, "Your Child's Brain," February 19, 1996). Sony issued a compact disc titled "Mozart Can Make You Smarter," and in Don Campbell's 1997 book of the same title, the term "The Mozart effect" was coined to refer to the impact of music stimulation on brain functions.

In response to the initial "Mozart effect" research, Flohr, Miller, and

Ways of Studying the Brain

SCANNING THE BRAIN

The **electroencephalogram** (EEG) detects and records brain waves from the surface of the skull and has yielded insight into normal brain development. This easily performed technique is not invasive and is appropriate for research involving young children. In EEG studies, the brain's electrical activity is recorded from the surface of the skull, using either paste-on electrodes or electrodes sewn into a cap. The EEG equipment detects small amounts of electrical energy and graphs brain waves. The frequency and intensity, or amplitude, of these brain waves indicate areas of the brain that are active.

Magnetic Resonance Imaging (MRI) and **Positron Emission Tomography (PET)** are primarily techniques used for diagnostic purposes. They have also yielded new insights into how the normal brain develops and functions. MRI produces detailed images of any internal body part. The functional MRI (fMRI) provides information about changes in the volume, flow, or oxygenation of blood that occurs as a person undertakes a task.

PET technology enables scientists to visualize fine details of the brain. It also determines levels of activity that are occurring in the various regions of the brain. Because PET scans require the injection of a tracer compound, parents of children not having medical problems are understandably reluctant to give consent for its use.

ANALYZING BRAIN CHEMISTRY

A useful, noninvasive way to study brain metabolism is to analyze chemicals involved in brain cell function. These chemicals can be found in various body fluids such as blood serum, urine, or saliva. Chemical analysis may become another valuable technique for studying the effects of music instruction on the brain functions of young children.

STUDYING THE BRAIN BEFORE BIRTH

High-resolution ultrasound measuring devices and recordings can be used by scientists to study and document early brain development of the child in the womb.

Note: For general information, see D. Hodges, "Neuromusical Research: A Review of the Literature," in D. Hodges, ed., *Handbook of Music Psychology,* San Antonio: Institute for Music Research, 1996.

Persellin conducted two new studies to evaluate the effects of music instruction on one aspect of cognition—visual spatial ability. The results were presented in papers titled "Children's Electrophysiological Responses to Music," at the 22nd International Society for Music Education World Conference, Amsterdam, 1996 (ERIC Document PS025654), and "Quantitative EEG Responses to Music Stimuli," at MENC's Biennial In-Service Conference, Phoenix, Arizona, 1998. Visual-spatial ability is used to form a mental representation of an object and supports such tasks as assembling jigsaw puzzles. In both studies, four- and five-year-old children from a preschool program were randomly divided into two groups, one of which received music instruction. The music instruction, which included singing, playing instruments, moving, listening, creating, and prereading/writing activities, took place for twenty-five minutes twice a week for seven weeks during the first study and over a ten-week period for the second study. In both studies, brain activity was measured by EEG, and differences were found between the two groups. The EEG results indicated that there was less electrical activity required to process spatial information in the brains of children who received the instruction, suggesting that their brain processing was more efficient.

Several new studies were brought to public attention last year. In one study ("The Effect of Music Training on Preschoolers' Spatial-Temporal Task Performance," *Journal of Research in Music Education,* vol. 46, no 1, 1998) Joyce Eastlund Gromko and Allison Smith Poorman found an increase in visual spatial ability in thirty three- and four-year-olds. These children received received thirty minutes a week of activity-based music instruction for seven months, and each child used a set of songbells. However, the differences that Gromko and Poorman observed were presented only in raw scores, not in results scaled for the children's ages.

In another study ("The McGill Piano Project: Effects of Three Years of Piano Instruction on Children's Cognitive Abilities, Academic Achievement, and Self-Esteem," paper presented at MENC's Biennial In-service Conference, Phoenix, Arizona, 1998), Eugenia Costa-Giomi found that weekly piano instruction significantly affected children's visual-spatial ability. During the children's first two years of study, the visual-spatial ability of those who received individual piano lessons increased significantly compared with that of children who did not. However, this increase was lost after the third year, implying that the effects were not permanent.

In a third study ("The Effect of Orff-based Music Instruction on the Spatial Temporal Skills of Young Children," paper presented at American Orff-Schulwerk Association national conference, Tampa, Florida, 1998), Diane C. Persellin found that forty-five minutes of intensive Orff-based music instruction three times a week initially produced a significant increase in the visual-spatial ability test scores of kindergartners. Like the Costa-Giomi study, however, the effect was transitory, and scores dropped six weeks after music instruction had ceased. All three of these studies measured differences using behavioral testing rather than EEG or other brain scanning devices.

Noted brain expert Eric Jensen writes in *Teaching with the Brain in Mind* (Association for Supervision and Curriculum Development, 1998) that a novice learner's brain is less efficient and, compared with the brain of an expert learner, "expends more energy" when confronted with a challenging task. Thus, if music instruction improves the ability to assemble puzzles (a visual-spatial skill), children who receive music instruction could be expected to expend less energy when attempting such tasks. The Flohr, Miller, and Persellin studies of 1996 and 1998, funded by the National Academy of Recording Arts and Sciences, indicated that children who received music instruction exerted less activity in the part of the brain associated with visual-spatial ability compared with others receiving no instruction. Although EEG differences were found between these groups of children, there were no differences in their spatial ability test scores. In order for behavioral performance changes to be noted, it may be necessary to make changes in future studies for such variables as length, frequency, and type of music instruction.

Techniques and Hypotheses

Even newer techniques than EEG are now available to assess the brain (see the sidebar). Functional magnetic resonance imaging (fMRI) and positron emission tomography (PET) are just two of the newer radiologic methods now used routinely in hospital settings. As the costs of these tests diminish, they can be applied in experimental settings. In addition, increasing knowledge of brain biochemistry has permitted study of brain cell metabolism through analysis of body fluids such as saliva. Although this technology is advancing rapidly, researchers have yet to establish the ideal setting and experimental conditions for these studies. There are many research questions that still need to be addressed: What is the optimal frequency and length of time for instruction? What are the most appropriate methods for assessment? What is the optimal age for intervention?

Music educators have long believed that music instruction is important to a child's brain development. Some of the basic tenets that have guided research are outlined in R. Shore's *Rethinking the Brain: New Insights into Early Development* (Families and Work Institute, 1997). We have adapted five hypotheses from this publication and have suggested a music education application for each:

- *The nature/nurture debate.* Human development hinges on the interplay between nature and nurture. Recent brain research challenges old assumptions about talent and innate ability. We do not necessarily come into the world with genes that determine how our brains develop. The impact of music education may be dramatic and specific, not merely influencing the general direction of development but also affecting the circuitry of the human brain.
- *The effects of nurture.* Early care and nurturing have a decisive, long-lasting impact on how people develop, their ability to learn, and their capacity to regulate their own emotions. Because of this, preschool education programs need to emphasize music as part of this care and nurturing.
- *Optimal music learning.* The human brain has a remarkable capacity to change, but timing is crucial. It appears that early childhood is a significant window of opportunity for music learning.
- *Minimal disadvantages.* The brain's plasticity also means that there are times when negative experiences or the absence of appropriate stimulation are more likely to have serious and sustained effects. Positive, stimulating preschool and elementary experiences like music education may help to counter some of these effects in young children.
- *The value of early music education.* Substantial evidence amassed by neuroscientists and child development experts over the last decade points to the wisdom and efficacy of early intervention. The findings indicate that all music educators and parents should be informed about the advantages of beginning music education with young children.

Researchers now are on the threshold of testing these hypotheses empirically. Improved technology will permit investigation of the impact of music on the child's brain. This could help us better understand not only spatial task ability but also other brain functions and intelligence as a whole.

John W. Flohr is professor of music at Texas Women's University (TWU) in Denton, Texas; Daniel C. Miller is professor of psychology at TWU; and Diane Persellin is professor of music at Trinity University in San Antonio, Texas.

The Effect of Music Training on Preschoolers' Spatial-Temporal Task Performance

Joyce Eastlund Gromko and Allison Smith Poorman

The purpose of this study was to investigate the effect of music training on preschoolers' Performance IQ (Wechsler Preschool and Primary Intelligence Scale–Revised, 1989). Preschoolers in the treatment group (N = 15) met weekly from October 1996 through April 1997. A Mann-Whitney test on Performance IQ (scaled) gain scores by group yielded U = 67, p = .059; a Mann-Whitney test on Performance IQ (raw) gain scores by group yielded U = 65, p = .049. Regressions of IQ gain scores on age showed significantly less gain for older children in the control group (N = 15). A regression analysis showed that the relationship of Performance IQ to age was not significant for the treatment group. Slopes intersected at age 3. For 3-year-olds in this study, an intellectually stimulating environment, per se, results in a gain in the ability to perform spatial-temporal tasks.

The results of recent psychological research, discussed widely in the popular press, emphasize the importance of an intellectually stimulating environment for the developing young child (see, for instance, Begley, 1996; Blakeslee, 1997; Zucker, 1994). On the basis of showing a significant effect for keyboard training on preschoolers' ability to assemble puzzles rapidly and accurately, psychologists concluded that music may be an important form of stimulation for the young child—one that generalizes to competencies outside music (Rauscher, Shaw, Levine, Wright, Dennis, & Newcomb, 1997).

In *The Psychology of the Child,* Piaget and Inhelder (1969) advanced a theory about how, through self-directed interactions with their environment, children construct knowledge. Given an environment in which children's intrinsic curiosity is nurtured, children grow more intelligent.

This chapter is reprinted from Joyce Eastlund Gromko and Allison Smith Poorman, "The Effect of Music Training on Preschoolers' Spatial-Temporal Task Performance," *Journal of Research in Music Education* 46, no. 2 (Summer 1998). Copyright 1998 by MENC.

Influenced by Piagetian thought, Gardner created a theory of intelligence that proposed seven separate "human competences" (Gardner, 1983, p. x), each with a distinctive developmental history (p. 64) and a distinctive symbol system (p. 66). Gardner sought to dispel the notion of intelligence as a general capacity (Gardner, 1983, p. ix). However, whether the seven human competences are separate, with distinctive developmental histories, or whether the intelligences are seven different manifestations of a general intelligence has not been established in the research.

Research has shown, not surprisingly, that music training leads to musical intelligence, the quality of which is reflected in children's invented symbols for musical sound (Bamberger, 1982, 1991; Davidson & Scripp, 1988, 1989; Domer & Gromko, 1996; Gromko, 1994, 1995a, 1995b, 1996a, 1996b, 1996c; Poorman, 1996; Smith, Cuddy, & Upitis, 1994). In other words, as children develop musical intelligence, their increasingly detailed perception of musical sound is reflected in their drawings and in the quality of their invented symbols for music. Furthermore, research has shown that music training that involves the child's motor system in kinesthetic responses improves children's musical perception (Flohr, 1981; Hurwitz, Wolff, Bortnick, & Kokas, 1975; Lewis, 1988; Metz, 1989; Morrongiello & Roes, 1990; Mueller, 1993). When children make music and move through space in response to music, children benefit musically.

Do children benefit spatially? This was the research question asked by Rauscher, Shaw, Levine, Wright, Dennis, and Newcomb (1997). Preschoolers in the keyboard treatment group showed significant gains on the ability to perform the Object Assembly, one subtest from the Wechsler Preschool and Primary Scale of Intelligence–Revised (WPPSI–R, 1989). Rauscher and her colleagues suggested that early music training may have effects that generalize beyond music to spatial-temporal tasks, lending empirical support to a theory of cortical development developed by Shaw and his colleagues at the University of California, Irvine (Shaw, Silverman, & Pearson, 1985).

An alternative theoretical basis for hypothesizing an effect of music training on spatial-temporal task performance derives from three similarities in the developmental histories of spatial and musical intelligence. First, the development of spatial and musical intelligence both depend on children's having sensory motor experiences. The connection between the motor system and spatial tasks is well-documented (Hardwick, McIntyre,

& Pick, 1976; Hintzman, O'Dell, & Arndt, 1981; Kozlowski & Bryant, 1977; Piaget & Inhelder, 1956; Presson & Hazelrigg, 1984; Presson & Montello, 1994; Rieser, 1989; Wohlschlaeger & Wohlschlaeger, 1998). For instance, research has shown that actual rotation of a body facilitates imagined rotation (Presson & Montello, 1994; Rieser, 1989) and actual rotation of a body is commensurate with imagined rotation (Wohlschlaeger & Wohlschlaeger, 1998). To the extent that musical training involves the motor system of young children, an effect on children's performance of spatial tasks might be predicted.

Second, it is also well-known that spatial memories have a hierarchical component (McNamara, 1986). Mental representations of spatial information are organized hierarchically, and these structures determine psychological distances between remembered locations (McNamara, Hardy, & Hirtle, 1989, p. 225). Huttenlocher, Jordan, and Levine (1994) found that children's ability to solve spatial problems is related to symbolic capacity and emerges around age 2. The structure of musical sound memory is also hierarchical (Gromko, 1994, 1995b, 1996b), as reflected in the progression of children's invented visual representations or symbols from global to increasingly detailed—from pulse to rhythmic pattern and from contour to functional pitches. The similar hierarchical structure of spatial and musical memories suggests commonalities in developmental histories for visual and aural perception.

Third, the effect of remembering temporal sequence strengthens memory for space, just as it assists memory for musical sound. Spatial memories preserve information about temporal sequence (McNamara, Halpin, & Hardy, 1992). When people learn a space, they encode both positions of objects and temporal-order information (p. 563). Likewise, when children encode music, they remember information about the temporal sequence of musical events and the relationship of pitches, motifs, and themes to one another.

The purpose of this study is to investigate the effect of music training on preschoolers' Performance IQ, using five spatial-temporal tasks from the Wechsler Preschool and Primary Intelligence Scale–Revised (1989), based on commonalities among spatial and musical developmental progressions. To test the theoretical foundation provided by research in spatial memory, a music treatment was designed that engaged children in sensory motor actions in response to music and assisted them in perception of and memory for music's tonal contour and rhythmic pulse.

Materials and Methods

Thirty-four preschool children from a private Montessori school in a midwestern city began the study, with 17 children in the treatment group and 17 in the control group. Parents from both groups provided written permission for their children to participate, with the understanding that any child could discontinue treatment at any point. After approximately 3 months, two preschoolers dropped out of the treatment group. Before analyses, two children, whose pretest Performance IQ was the same as that of the children who discontinued treatment, were removed from the control group in order to assure matched Performance IQ means at the outset. Thus, 30 3- and 4-year-olds completed the study, with 15 in each group.

The first author designed and taught the music treatment, assisted by the second author. Preschoolers in the treatment group met from 3:20 P.M. until 3:50 P.M. on 24 Tuesdays, from October 1, 1996, to April 29, 1997. Every family purchased a 20-note set of songbells, consisting of chromatic metal bars from middle C to the G an octave and a half above; this instrument was kept at home for practice. Each week, children took a practice plan home so parents could guide their children's practice. Silver Burdett Ginn (1991, 1995) granted the authors permission to make taped copies of recordings of music; every child received a tape of songs, to be played and sung between music sessions.

A new song, limited in range and numbers of pitches, was presented at each session. The sessions were designed to involve the children's motor systems in response to musical sound, to draw their attention to pitch and rhythmic aspects of songs, and to increase their memory for musical sound. Therefore, children (a) sang the new song several times; (b) accompanied their singing with body percussion that "painted" the melody in the air and established the music's steady pulse; (c) took turns playing a simplified version of the song on songbells or hand chimes; (d) made a picture of the song using round stickers on a paper; and (e) followed a tactile touch chart that outlined the contour of the song. In addition, two familiar songs were danced and sung.

A research assistant, assisted by the second author, conducted all the Performance IQ testing for all children. When necessary, teachers at the school accompanied shy children into the testing room. The first author, who analyzed the data, was not involved in testing.

All children were pretested on the WPPSI–R spatial-temporal tasks in September 1996 and posttested in May 1997. About the purposes and uses of the WPPSI–R, Wechsler (1989) explains:

> The WPPSI–R is intended for use as a measure of intellectual ability in a wide range of educational, clinical, and research settings.... The WPPSI–R may also be used in studies to document change in performance over time and to measure the effects of manipulation. (p. 8)

Concerning reliability, Wechsler states, "The WPPSI–R is a highly reliable instrument, especially at the level of the IQ scores" (p. 130). Performance IQ score is the sum of scores on five subtests. Wechsler suggests, "If one of the Performance subtest scores cannot be used, Animal Pegs may be administered as an alternate" (p. 25); therefore, we substituted Animal Pegs for mazes, because several of the children in our study could not grip or use a pencil with facility. Thus, the five subtests we used were Object Assembly, Geometric Design, Block Design, Picture Completion, and Animal Pegs. For the Object Assembly task, children constructed six puzzles, two within a frame and four freestanding. In Geometric Design, children chose a matching geometric design from an array of four geometric designs, and they drew geometric designs with a pencil. For the Block Design task, children constructed a red and white shape from square blocks using a picture as a model. For the Picture Completion task, children pointed at what was missing in the picture. Animal Pegs required children to associate colored pegs with pictures of animals and to systematically fill in holes row by row.

Subtest scores were recorded as raw scores and a Performance IQ (raw) was calculated, with a mean of 100 and a standard deviation of 15. About the interpretation of raw scores, Wechsler (1989) explains:

> The Verbal, Performance, and Full Scale IQ distribution each has a mean of 100 and a standard deviation of 15 ... IQs of 85 and 115 correspond to 1 standard deviation below and above the mean, respectively, whereas IQs of 70 and 130 are each 2 standard deviations from the mean. About two-thirds of all children obtain IQs between 85 and 115, about 95 percent score in the 70 to 130 range, and nearly all obtain IQs between 55 and 145 (3 standard deviations on either side of the mean). (p. 124)

Raw scores on subtests were converted to scaled scores, "consistent with the theory underlying the Wechsler scales that the child be compared with his or her chronological age peers" (p. 122), and a Performance IQ (scaled) was computed.

Results

The Performance IQ (scaled) pretest mean was 61.00 ($SD = 11.95$) for the control group and 60.87 ($SD = 12.26$) for the treatment group; the Performance IQ (scaled) posttest mean was 67.73 for the control group ($SD = 7.02$) and 72.47 ($SD = 9.34$) for the treatment group. Performance IQ (raw) pretest mean for the control group was 116.40 ($SD = 18.13$) and for the treatment group was 116.40 ($SD = 18.52$); the Performance IQ (raw) posttest mean for the control group was 125.64 ($SD = 11.47$) and for the treatment group was 134.00 ($SD = 14.91$). Because we were interested in comparing the gain in Performance IQ over 8 months, gain scores (posttest-pretest) for Performance IQ (scaled) and Performance IQ (raw) were calculated for the control and treatment groups. A Mann-Whitney test on Performance IQ (scaled) gain scores by group yielded $U = 67$, $p = .059$. A Mann-Whitney on Performance IQ (raw) gain scores by group yielded $U = 65$, $p = .049$. The treatment group made significantly more gain in raw scores than the control group.

A regression of Performance IQ (scaled) gain scores on age ($y = 39.43 - 7.97x$) was significant, $F (1, 13) = 10.30$, $p = .007$, for the control group. That is, the gain in Performance IQ (scaled) for preschoolers in the control group was less for older children. Whereas the sign of the slope for the treatment group was also negative ($y = 27.21 - 4.24x$), the relationship of Performance IQ (scaled) to age was not significant, $F (1, 13) = .89$, n.s. A regression of Performance IQ (raw) gain scores on age yielded similar results, with the sign of each slope negative (control: $y = 56.50 - 11.45x$; and treatment: $y = 39.11 - 5.84x$) and the effect of age significant, $F (1, 13) = 8.72$, $p = .01$, for the control group only.

Discussion

Whereas influential theories in spatial knowledge do not make specific predictions about the effect of music training on spatial-temporal task performance, the principles derived from investigations into the nature of spatial memories provide a rationale for the effects of music training on spatial knowledge (Baenninger & Newcombe, 1995; Huttenlocher, Jordan, & Levine, 1994; Huttenlocher & Presson, 1979; McNamara, Halpin, & Hardy, 1992; McNamara, Hardy, & Hirtle, 1989; Presson & Montello, 1994). Our results show that when the Performance IQ gain scores (scaled and raw) were regressed on age the slopes intersected at age

3, suggesting that for the 3-year-olds in our study, an intellectually stimulating environment results in a gain in the ability to perform spatial-temporal tasks. However, the regressions showed that music training held the gain steady for older preschoolers in the treatment group, whereas without music training, the gains decreased significantly for children in the control group.

We suggest the reader interpret our results with caution, given the close disparity between alpha levels for raw and scaled Performance IQ gain scores. Our findings would be strengthened by increasing the size of our sample, lengthening the time of our treatment, and sampling other types of preschool or daycare environments. Our subjects were drawn from a private Montessori school, where all children learn within an intellectually stimulating environment, receive a "traditional" music class for 30 minutes every week, and benefit from outside activities provided by their parents. On the basis of these results, therefore, we cannot assert that music treatment is the only way to boost young children's intelligence. However, given that both groups were drawn from intellectually stimulating environments, that the music treatment group showed a significantly higher mean gain on the Performance IQ (raw), and that the gain held steady across ages within the treatment group, we believe music training can have a positive effect on the development of spatial intelligence in preschool children.

Implications for Music Education

While it has been acknowledged in scholarly and popular publications that rich, engaging, and active experiences are critical for a child's cognitive development, little has been done to assure that the home and school environments for all young children are intellectually stimulating and conducive to growth in musical and spatial intelligence. Research in music education has traditionally been concerned with school-age children. We believe that early music training with an emphasis on sensory motor activity, visual and aural perception of space and sound, and the improvement of memory for space and sound nurtures a young child's intrinsic love of learning, helps them move expressively and perceptively within their environments, and sustains and encourages their intellectual growth up to the point that they enter school. We recommend that further research be conducted with larger and more diverse groups of children to determine the effect of early music training on children's sensory motor coordination, visual and aural perception of their environment, and duration and accuracy of spatial and musical memory. We recommend that research collaborations be constructed across fields of inquiry (e.g., music, early childhood education, and experimental and clinical psychology) and that researchers work with practitioners and parents to improve the early education of preschoolers.

References

Baenninger, M., & Newcombe, N. (1995). Environmental input to the development of sex-related differences in spatial and mathematical ability. *Learning and Individual Differences, 7* (4), 363–379.

Bamberger, J. (1982). Revisiting children's drawings of simple rhythms: A function for reflection-in-action. In S. Strauss (Ed.), *U-shaped behavioral growth* (pp. 191–226). New York: Academic Press.

Bamberger, J. (1991). *The mind behind the musical ear: How children develop musical intelligence.* Cambridge, MA: Harvard University Press.

Begley, S. (1996, February 19). Your child's brain. *Newsweek,* pp. 55–57, 61–62.

Blakeslee, S. (1997, April 17). Studies show talking with infants shapes basis of ability to think. *The New York Times,* A14.

Davidson, L., & Scripp, L. (1988). Young children's musical representations. Windows on music cognition. In J. A. Sloboda (Ed.), *Generative processes in music: The psychology of performance improvisation and composition* (pp. 195–230). New York: Oxford University Press.

Davidson, L., & Scripp, L. (1989). Education and development in music from a cognitive perspective. In D. J. Hargreaves (Ed.), *Children and the arts.* Milton Keynes, England: Open University Press.

Domer, J., & Gromko, J. (1996). Qualitative changes in preschoolers' invented notations following music instruction. *Contributions to Music Education, 23,* 62–78.

Flohr, J. W. (1981). Short-term music instruction and young children's developmental music aptitude. *Journal of Research in Music Education, 29,* 219–223.

Gardner, H. (1983). *Frames of mind.* New York: Basic Books.

Gromko, J. E. (1994). Children's invented notations as measures of musical understanding. *Psychology of Music, 22,* 136-147.

Gromko, J. E. (1995a). *Origins of symbolic intelligence.* Paper presented at Symposium for Research in General Music, University of Arizona, Tucson.

Gromko, J. E. (1995b). Discovered literacy. *The Orff Echo, 28* (1), 24–29.

Gromko, J. E. (1996a, May). *Early signs of musical intelligence.* Paper presented at the Qualitative Methodologies Conference II, University of Illinois, Urbana–Champaign.

Gromko, J. E. (1996b, July). *A theory of symbolic development in music.* Paper presented at the International Society of Music Education conference, Amsterdam, Holland.

Gromko, J. E. (1996c). In a child's voice: Interpretive interactions with young composers. *Bulletin of the Council for Research in Music Education,* no. 128, 37–58.

Hardwick, D. A., McIntyre, C. W., & Pick, H. L., Jr. (1976). The content and manipulation of cognitive maps in children and adults. *Monographs for the Society for Research in Child Development,* entire issue, no. 166.

Hintzman, D., O'Dell, C., & Arndt, D. (1981). Orientations in cognitive maps. *Cognitive Psychology, 13,* 149–206.

Hurwitz, I., Wolff, P. H., Bortnick, B. D., & Kokas, K. (1975). Nonmusical effects of the Kodály music curriculum in primary grade children. *Journal of Learning Disabilities, 8* (3), 167–174.

Huttenlocher, J., Jordan, N. C., & Levine, S. C. (1994). A mental model for early arithmetic. *Journal of Experimental Psychology: General, 123* (3), 284–296.

Huttenlocher, J., & Presson, C. C. (1979). The coding and transformation of spatial information. *Cognitive Psychology, 11,* 375–394.

Kozlowski, L., & Bryant, K. (1977). Sense of direction, spatial orientation, and cognitive maps. *Journal of Experimental Psychology: Human Perception and Performance, 3,* 590–598.

Lewis, B. (1988). The effect of movement-based instruction on first- and third-graders' achievement in selected music listening skills. *Psychology of Music, 16* (2), 128–142.

McNamara, T. P. (1986). Mental representations of spatial relations. *Cognitive Psychology, 18,* 87–121.

McNamara, T. P., Halpin, J. A., & Hardy, J. K. (1992). Spatial and temporal contributions to the structure of spatial memory. *Journal of Experimental Psychology: Learning, Memory, and Cognition, 19* (3), 555–564.

McNamara, T. P., Hardy, J. K., & Hirtle, S. C. (1989). Subjective hierarchies in spatial memory. *Journal of Experimental Psychology: Learning, Memory, and Cognition, 15* (2), 211–227.

Metz, E. (1989). Movement as a musical response among preschool children. *Journal of Research in Music Education, 37,* 48–60.

Morrongiello, B. A., & Roes, C. L. (1990). Developmental changes in children's perception of musical sequences: Effects of musical training. *Developmental Psychology, 26* (5), 814–820.

Mueller, A. (1993). *The effect of movement-based instruction on the melodic per-*

ception of primary-age general music students. Unpublished doctoral dissertation, Arizona State University, Tempe.

Piaget, J., & Inhelder, B. (1956). *A child's conception of space.* New York: Routledge and Kegan Paul.

Piaget, J., & Inhelder, B. (1969). *The psychology of the child.* New York: Basic Books.

Poorman, A. S. (1996). The emergence of symbol use: Prekindergarten children's representations of musical sound. *Contributions to Music Education, 23,* 31–45.

Presson, C., & Hazelrigg, M. (1984). Building spatial representations through primary and secondary learning. *Journal of Experimental Psychology: Learning, Memory, and Cognition, 10* (4), 716–722.

Presson, C., & Montello, D. (1994). Updating after rotational and translational body movements: Coordinate structure of perspective space. *Perception, 23* (12), 1447–1455.

Rauscher, F., Shaw, G., Levine, L., Wright, E., Dennis, W., & Newcomb, R. (1997). Music training causes long-term enhancement of preschool children's spatial-temporal reasoning. *Neurological Research, 19* (1), 2–8.

Rieser, J. J. (1989). Access to knowledge of spatial structure at novel points of observation. *Journal of Experimental Psychology: Learning, Memory, and Cognition, 15* (6), 1157–1165.

Shaw, G., Silverman, D., & Pearson, J. (1985). Model of cortical organization embodying a basis for a theory of information processing and memory recall. *Proceedings of the National Academy of Sciences, 82,* 2364–2368.

Silver Burdett Ginn. (1991). *World of music. Grades K–1.* Morristown, NJ: Author.

Silver Burdett Ginn. (1995). *The music connection. Grades K–1.* Needham, MA: Author.

Smith, K. C., Cuddy, L. L., & Upitis, R. (1994). Figural and metric understanding of rhythm. *Psychology of Music, 22,* 117–135.

Wechsler, D. (1989). *Preschool and Primary Scale of Intelligence–Revised.* San Antonio, TX: The Psychological Corporation.

Wohlschlaeger, A., & Wohlschlaeger, A. (1998). Mental and manual rotation. *Journal of Experimental Psychology: Human Perception and Performance, 24* (2), 397–412.

Zucker, J. (Executive Producer). (1994, October 17). *The Today Show.* New York: National Broadcasting Co.

Joyce Eastlund Gromko is associate dean for academic affairs in the Graduate College and associate professor of music education in the College of Musical Arts at Bowling Green State University (BGSU) in Bowling Green, Ohio. Allison Smith Poorman is assistant director of creative arts at BGSU.

Academic Achievement

SAT Scores of Students in the Arts

Sue Rarus

MENC has tracked SAT scores of music students for a number of years. Drawing on data published by the College Board, MENC has summarized the positive correlations between coursework/experience in music and above-average SAT scores (see, for example, the October 1995 and October 1999 "FYI" columns in Teaching Music). *The latest summary, shown here, is also available on MENC's Web site at www.menc.org.*

Students of the arts continue to outperform their nonarts peers on the Scholastic Assessment Test (SAT), according to reports by the College Entrance Examination Board. In 1999, SAT takers with coursework/experience in music performance scored 53 points higher on the verbal portion of the test and 39 points higher on the math portion than students with no coursework or experience in the arts. Scores for those with coursework in music appreciation were 61 points higher on the verbal and 42 points higher on the math portion.

Data for these reports were gathered by the College Board from the Student Descriptive Questionnaire, a voluntary component of the SAT that provides self-reported information about students' academic participation.

Years of Study	Verbal Mean Scores		Math Mean Scores	
	1998	1999	1998	1999
4 or more Years	538	538	533	537
3 Years	514	515	514	513
2 Years	506	506	512	511
1 Year	498	498	510	508
.5 Year or Less	488	487	501	499

Course Title	Verbal Mean Scores		Math Mean Scores	
	1998	1999	1998	1999
Acting/Play Production	543	543	533	532
Art History/ Appreciation	518	518	518	517
Dance	513	514	509	508
Drama: Study or Appreciation	533	534	522	521
Music:Study or Appreciation	537	538	535	534
Music Performance	529	530	530	531
Photography/Film	525	526	524	524
Studio Art/Design	524	525	527	527
No Arts Coursework	477	477	494	492

Sources: The College Board, *Profile of College-Bound Seniors National Report* for 1998 and 1999.

Sue Rarus is information services manager at MENC—The National Association for Music Education.

The Effects of Three Years of Piano Instruction on Children's Cognitive Development

Eugenia Costa-Giomi

The relationship between music and cognitive abilities was studied by observing the cognitive development of children provided (n = 63) and not provided (n = 54) with individual piano lessons from fourth to sixth grade. There were no differences in cognitive abilities, musical abilities, motor proficiency, self-esteem, academic achievement, or interest in studying piano between the two groups of children at the beginning of the study. It was found that the treatment affected children's general and spatial cognitive development. The magnitude of such effects (omega squared) was small. Additional analyses showed that although the experimental group obtained higher spatial abilities scores in the Developing Cognitive Abilities Test after 1 and 2 years of instruction than did the control group, the groups did not differ in general or specific cognitive abilities after 3 years of instruction. The treatment did not affect the development of quantitative and verbal cognitive abilities.

Experienced musicians and musically talented individuals differ from nonmusicians in the development of specific cognitive abilities and in certain aspects of brain structure and functioning (Barrett & Barker, 1973; Besson, Faita, & Requin, 1994; Bever & Chiarello, 1974; Hassler, 1992; Hassler, Birbaumer, & Feil, 1985; Hassler & Nieschlag, 1989; Johnson, Petsche, Richter, von Stein, & Filz, 1996; Manturzewska, 1978; Schlaug, Amunts, Janke, & Zilles, 1996; Schlaug, Jancke, Hung, & Steinmetz, 1995). It has been found that, in general, musicians obtain higher scores in tests of spatial abilities than do subjects with no music training (Barret & Barker, 1973; Gromko & Poorman, 1998; Hassler & Nieschlag, 1989; Hassler, 1992; Hurwitz, Wolff, Bortnick, & Kokas,

This chapter is reprinted from Eugenia Costa-Giomi, "The Effects of Three Years of Piano Instruction on Children's Cognitive Development," *Journal of Research in Music Education* 47, no. 3 (Fall 1999). Copyright 1999 by MENC. (This study was funded by a grant from the National Piano Foundation.)

1975; Karma, 1979; Manturzewska, 1978; Philbrick & Mallory, 1996; Rauscher, Shaw, et al., 1997). Many of these studies' conclusions were based on correlations between spatial and musical abilities or comparisons between musicians and nonmusicians, raising questions about the type of relationship that exists between these abilities. Is the possession of strong spatial abilities a required characteristic for success in music, or does music instruction improve the development of spatial abilities?

Some studies in which a musical treatment was provided as a controlled condition showed an improvement in specific spatial abilities in rats (Rauscher, Robinson, & Jens, 1997) and humans (Gromko & Poorman, 1998; Philbrick & Mallory, 1996; Rauscher, Shaw, & Ky, 1993; 1995; Rauscher, Shaw, Levine, Ky, & Wright, 1994; Rauscher, Shaw, et al., 1997; Rideaut, Dougherty, & Wernert, 1998; Rideout & Taylor, 1997). Other studies, however, failed to find such improvements (Newman et al., 1995; Stough, Kerkin, Bates, & Mangan, 1994). In most investigations, the musical intervention ranged from short listening sessions to 7 months of daily music instruction. Invariably, the studies providing music instruction were conducted with young children. The results of most of these studies showed that children participating in music instruction outperformed children not receiving formal music instruction in one of the five scales of the Performance Wechsler Preschool and Primary Scale of Intelligence–Revised (WPPSI–R), namely the Object Assembly Scale (Philbrick & Mallory, 1996; Rauscher et al. 1994; Rauscher, Shaw, et al., 1997). The music treatment did not affect children's scores in the other Performance Scales of the WPPSI–R, such as Geometric Design, Block Design, and Picture Completion. Only Gromko and Poorman (1998) found an effect of music instruction on children's total raw scores in the Performance WPPSI–R. Interestingly, investigators in an earlier study of the effects of 7 months of daily music instruction on first-graders' spatial abilities found that the treatment did not affect children's scores in the Object Assembly Scale of the Wechsler Intelligence Scale for Children (WISC), but improved their scores in the Children's Embedded Figures Test, the Graham Kendall Memory for Designs Test, the Raven Progressive Matrices, and the Block Design subtest of the WISC (Hurwitz et al., 1975).

It is unclear which types of spatial abilities are affected by music instruction, and it is also unknown whether the improvement in spatial abilities is long-lasting. Research has been based on behavioral observations of cognitive changes gathered immediately after the treatment or within a few days of its conclusion, calling into question the long-term effects of music instruction on cognitive development. In fact, some of the reported changes in cognitive abilities attributed to music treatments lasted no more than 15 minutes (Rauscher et al., 1993). If there is a neurophysiological basis for the behavioral effects of music on cognitive development, one would expect these effects to be permanent. Unfortunately, there are no longitudinal behavioral studies on this problem and scarce neurological research on the origins of these effects.

Sarnthein et al. (1997) used coherence analysis of electroencephalograms (EEG) to study adults who listened to music or text and then completed a spatial task to investigate the neurological basis of the relationship between spatial cognitive development and music exposure. The data from two of the eight subjects participating in the study suggest that listening to music had a positive carryover effect on the mental processes involved in the spatial task by increasing the functional efficacy of certain neural centers. This evidence is tempered by the lack of explanation regarding the improvement in spatial scores of the other subjects, for whom apparently no music carryover effects were noticed. In addition, the effect of task order was not examined; this begs the question as to whether the improved performance in the spatial task was caused by repeated testing or by the musical intervention.

One of the problems of conducting longitudinal studies on the effects of learning music is the selection of comparable experimental and control groups. Subjects who undertake and persist in music instruction might differ from those who never seek to participate or from those who drop out of music lessons. A survey conducted by Duke, Flowers, and Wolfe (1997) in 30 states in the United States to profile students and families who participate in piano instruction showed that most piano students are Caucasian (80%), female (70%), from upper-middle income (44% reported family incomes greater than $70,000, 39% reported incomes between $40,000 and $70,000, and 18% reported incomes below $40,000), have well-educated parents (80% of mothers and fathers hold at least one college degree), and live at home with both parents (84%). The privileged environment of the typical piano student is striking. In addition to differences in demographic and family characteristics between students who study music and those who do not participate in formal music instruction, other motivational differences might exist between the two groups. It is possible that the interests and perseverance of the students who take instrumental lessons for an extensive period of time reflect other personal differences between the groups. Whether these differences affect the relationship of cognitive development and music instruction is unknown. The present study controlled for some of these differences and explored their possible impact on the development of cognitive abilities in children participating in formal music instruction.

The present longitudinal study focused on the nonmusical effects of piano instruction in children. This article reports the results regarding the effects of 3 years of piano instruction on children's cognitive abilities. The profile of the children participating in the study was quite different from the profile of a typical piano student as described by Duke et al. (1997); the goal was to examine whether music instruction affects the cognitive abilities of children from less-privileged backgrounds.

Method

Subjects

During the summer semester of 1994, a letter describing this project was sent to the parents ($n = 698$) of all fourth-grade children (all were 9 years old) attending the 20 English-language schools of the largest school board (this corresponds to a school district in the United States) in Montreal, Quebec. Parents of 289 children stated interest in the project. Of the parents who did not respond to the letter, 43 were contacted by phone and 74 by mail to confirm that respondents and nonrespondents did not differ in demographic characteristics relevant to the investigation. A total of 117 children (58 girls and 59 boys) participated in the study. Their parents gave informed consent prior to the start of the intervention. These children had never participated in formal music instruction, did not have a piano at home, and their family income was below $40,000 (approximately $30,000 in U.S. dollars) per annum. Sixty-seven children from 11 schools were assigned to the experimental group (the group receiving piano lessons), and 50 children from 12 schools were assigned to the control group (the group not receiving piano lessons). Because of ethical concerns (such as parents and children feeling discriminated for not being provided with piano lessons) and scheduling conflicts, three schools did not have a control group and four schools did not have an experimental group. In the experimental group, 38% of the children lived with a single parent, while 28% did so in the control group. Approximately half the families had one adult with a full-time or part-time job (51% in the experimental group and 54% in the control group). The proportion of families in the experimental and control groups with unemployed parents was 30% and 22%, respectively. Of these families, 97% reported income from welfare subsidies of less than $20,000 (Canadian). Approximately half the children in each group were boys (49% in the experimental and 51% in the control group).

The sample from the school ($n = 20$) attended by 10 children who dropped out of the piano lessons was not included in the analyses because the preservation of the randomness of the remaining sample was questionable. The 11 children from other schools who discontinued piano instruction during the 3 years of the treatment but completed all required testing were included as part of the experimental group. Possible differences among the children who dropped out of instruction, those who completed 3 years of piano instruction, and those who never partici-pated in formal music instruction were investigated. Additionally, nine children (three from the experimental group and six from the control group) moved to another city during the 3 years of the study and did not complete the required testing. Because the reason for their withdrawal from the project was unrelated to the treatment, no further analyses were performed on the incomplete data of this group of children. If a child missed one of the multiple administrations of a specific test, the child's remaining scores in this test were not analyzed. This procedure was nec-essary to allow for the repeated-measures statistical analysis performed with the data. A total of 78 children (35 in the control group and 43 in the experimental group) completed all cognitive abilities tests.

TREATMENT

Each child in the experimental group received, at no cost to the fami-lies, 3 years of piano instruction and an acoustic piano. Nine teachers (six female and three male) provided children with individual piano lessons weekly. Lessons were held at the participating schools during lunch recess or after school hours. The lessons were 30 minutes long during the first 2 years, and 45 minutes in length during the third year. Teachers followed a traditional curriculum based on the development of basic techniques and repertoire from simple popular melodies to classical sonatinas.

TESTING

Prior to the treatment, children in both the control and experimental groups were administered five standardized tests with adequate reliability levels for the age of the sample: Level E of the Developing Cognitive Abilities Test (DCAT), the tonal and rhythmic audiation subtests of the Musical Aptitude Profile, the fine motor subtests of the Bruininks-Oseretsky Test of Motor Proficiency, the language and mathematics subtests Level 14 of the Canadian Achievement Test 2 (CAT2), and the Coopersmith Self-Esteem Inventories (long form). At the end of the first, second, and third years of instruction, children took the appropriate level of the DCAT (i.e., levels E, F, and G, respectively) and the self-esteem test. At the end of the second and third years, children also took the language and math subtests of the CAT2. Tests were administered to mixed groups of experimental and control subjects in the same order in all schools. The testing sessions were scheduled during the morning and with appropriate breaks within each session. The only individual test was the motor proficiency test. According to the results of independent *t*-tests, there were no differences between the scores of the control and experimental groups in any of the five standardized tests administered prior to the beginning of the treatment.

The piano teachers completed weekly progress reports with the collaboration of the children. These reports provided information about children's attendance to the lessons and their practice routine during the 3 years of instruction.

Results

To study the effect of the music treatment on children's cognitive development, a series of analyses comparing the control and experimental groups was performed. Another set of analyses compared the cognitive development of three groups of children: those who completed the 3 years of treatment, those who never participated in formal music instruction, and those who dropped out of the lessons. This second set of analyses was done to determine whether the differences between the control and experimental groups found in the first series of analyses were the result of a process of attrition during which less-capable children dropped out of the treatment. The third set of analyses added a number of additional independent variables to the model: sex, income, family structure (single- or two-parent family), and parental employment. These variables could not be included simultaneously because of certain redundancy in the information. For example, all families with unemployed parents had incomes of less than $20,000 (Canadian). Finally, certain exploratory analyses, such as regression analyses, were performed.

The total cognitive abilities scores (dependent variable) of the control and experimental groups (between-subjects variable) in 1994, 1995, 1996, and 1997 (i.e., Year, within-subjects variable) were compared through an analysis of variance (ANOVA) with repeated measures. The interaction between Group and Year was significant, $F(3, 228) = 3.90$, adjusted G–G $p = .01$. Tukey comparisons indicated significant differences in the scores of the control and experimental groups after 2 years of instruction ($p = .05$). There were no differences between the groups prior to the treatment and after 1 and 3 years of instruction (Figure 1).

To determine which types of cognitive abilities were affected by the treatment, three analyses of variance (ANOVAs) with repeated measures were performed on the three subtests of the cognitive abilities test: verbal, quantitative, and spatial. Group (between-subjects variable) and Year (within-subjects variable) were the independent variables, and subtest

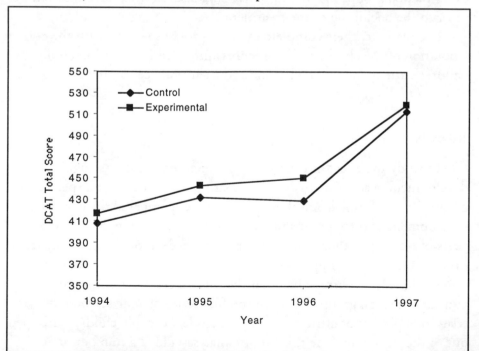

Figure 1. Control and experimental groups' general cognitive abilities scores.

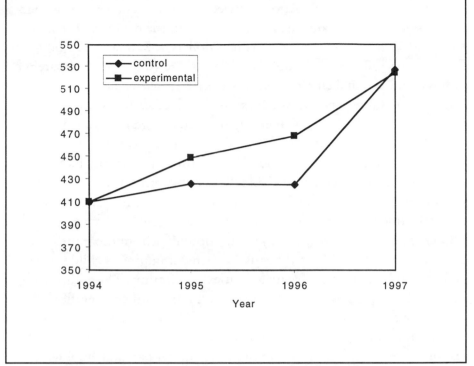

Figure 2. Control and experimental groups' spatial abilities scores.

scores was the dependent variable. A significant interaction between Group and Year was found for the spatial subtest scores, $F(3, 228) = 5.28$, adj. G-G $p < .01$. Tukey comparisons indicated that the experimental group's spatial scores were higher than those of the control group after 1 and 2 years of instruction ($p = .05$) and that the groups' spatial scores did not differ prior to the treatment or after 3 years of piano lessons (Figure 2).

The interaction of Group and Year was not significant in the analyses of the quantitative and verbal abilities, suggesting that the musical intervention had no effect on the development of these abilities. The significant effects of the music treatment on general cognitive abilities and spatial abilities were studied in more detail by determining the magnitude of these effects. The omega-squared value, which provides a relative measure of the size of a variable effect, was used for this purpose. The omega-squared value for the effects of the music treatment on general cognitive abilities was .02, and for those on spatial abilities, .04. According to

Keppel (1982), values of less than .06 are considered small in the behavioral and social sciences.

To study possible interactions between relevant demographic characteristics of the sample and the music treatment, the data was reanalyzed to include gender, income (in Canadian dollars, < $20,000; $20,000–$30,000; or $30,000–$40,000), family structure (single- or two-parent family), and parental employment (0, 1, or 2 employed adults in the household) as independent variables. As described earlier, these variables could not be included simultaneously because of certain redundancy in the information. Separate ANOVAs with repeated measures, including Group (between-subjects variable), Year (within-subjects variable), and one additional independent variable (between-subjects variable), were conducted on children's total scores in the DCAT. Similar analyses were also performed on children's spatial, verbal, and quantitative scores in the DCAT. The results of these analyses did not differ from those presented earlier, as they showed that the music treatment improved children's general cognitive abilities and spatial abilities significantly. The additional independent variables did not interact with the treatment significantly for any of the test scores, suggesting that the temporal effects of the music intervention on cognitive development occurred in the children regardless of the sex, family income, family structure, or parental employment.

Another set of ANOVAs with repeated measures followed by Tukey comparisons was performed to study possible differences in the cognitive abilities of children who dropped out of the treatment ($n = 11$) and those in the experimental ($n = 32$) and control groups ($n = 35$). It was found that the experimental group obtained higher general and spatial scores than did the control group after 2 years of instruction ($p = .05$) and that there were no differences between the dropout and control groups or between the dropout and experimental groups for any of the DCTA scores. This indicates that the differences between the experimental and control groups reported earlier are not the result of a process of attrition during which children with lower cognitive abilities discontinued their participation in piano instruction and those with higher abilities continued taking the piano lessons, but are likely due to the treatment.

A question that seemed relevant to consider was whether the effects of piano instruction on cognitive abilities were dependent on children's efforts in learning to play the piano. Because the children in this study did not seek to engage themselves in music instruction but were solicited directly to take piano lessons, they probably came to the study with diverse levels of motivation in learning music. A series of exploratory analyses was performed with the data collected through the weekly piano progress reports of the children in the experimental group. From these reports, it was possible to calculate the number of lessons children missed per year and the average time in minutes they practiced per week. These two types of observations, which reflected children's dedication to learning the piano, were included in multiple regression analyses as the independent variables. The differences between the pretest scores (verbal, quantitative, spatial, and total) and the scores obtained after 1, 2, and 3 years of instruction were calculated for each child in the experimental group and included in the analyses as the dependent variables. To include the partial data from children who had dropped out of the lessons, multiple regression analyses were performed with the cumulative data of children who completed 1 ($n = 61$), 2 ($n = 42$), and 3 ($n = 38$) years of instruction. Significant results were found only for the multiple regression of general cognitive abilities and spatial abilities of the children who completed 3 years of piano lessons, $F(2, 37) = 4.82$, $p = .01$, and $F(2, 37) = 4.76$, $p = .01$, respectively. Effort to learn the piano, as measured by lessons missed and average practice time per week, explained 21% of the variance in spatial abilities and 22% of the variance in total cognitive abilities after 3 years of piano instruction. No significant results were found in the multiple-regression analyses of children who completed 1 and 2 years of instruction.

Discussion

The results of the study show that the treatment improved children's general cognitive abilities and spatial abilities significantly but that these improvements were only temporary. After 2 years of piano instruction, children in the experimental group obtained significantly higher total scores in the cognitive abilities test than did the children in the control group. The spatial scores of the experimental group were also significantly higher than were those of the control group after 1 and 2 years of individual piano lessons. However, no differences in cognitive abilities were found between the groups after 3 years of instruction, calling into question the long-term effects of the treatment on cognitive development. The same results were obtained when children's sex, family income, family structure (single- or two-parent family), and parental employment were taken into account, suggesting that the temporary effects of the music treatment on cognitive development were not dependent upon these factors. It was also found that individual piano instruction did not affect the development of children's quantitative and verbal cognitive abilities, providing further evidence that the contribution of music instruction to cognitive development might be more limited than has been previously suggested.

Other findings of the study that point to the limitations of the cognitive benefits of the treatment were those regarding the magnitude of the effects (i.e., omega squared). The calculation of the magnitude, which represents the relative size or strength of the treatment effects, yielded values considered low in the behavioral and social sciences (Keppel, 1982). In other words, the temporary improvements in cognitive abilities produced by the treatment, even if significant, were small.

The explanation of these results is difficult because they seem to present conflicting information. On the one hand, the cognitive improvements found after 1 and 2 years of treatment support the idea that music instruction produces neurological changes that in turn improve certain types of cognitive abilities. On the other hand, no cognitive improvements were found after the 3 year of treatment. If it is true that music instruction produces modifications in children's neural processes, one would expect the cognitive improvements to be permanent.

Why did the positive effects of the treatment provided in this study fade after 2 years? I propose that the positive effects of the treatment were dependent upon children's dedication to learning piano. The evidence I have is based on the analysis of the piano progress reports of the children in the experimental group. After 3 years of treatment, 22% of the variance in cognitive improvements of the children receiving piano instruction was explained by their attendance at the lessons and time spent practicing piano. This suggests that children who persisted and participated more actively in the process of learning the piano benefitted to a greater extent than did those less likely to attend the lessons and practice. However, it is important to mention that these factors did not explain the cognitive improvements within the experimental group during the first 2 years of treatment. If these results, which are based on differences *within* the experimental group, are compared with those reported earlier based on differences *between* the experimental and control groups, one will notice an interesting contrast. During the initial 2 years of treatment, differences in cognitive abilities were evident between the control and experimental groups, indicating that the treatment affected children's cognitive development. Additionally, during these 2 years, no effects on cognitive development resulting from dedication to learning the piano were detected within the experimental group. However, after the initial 2 years, no differences in cognitive abilities between the control and experimental groups were found, whereas cognitive development was affected within the experimental group by dedication to learning piano. At the beginning of the project, when children were enthusiastic about the new activity and acquired piano skills faster and more easily, their cognitive abilities improved. After the initial enthusiasm disappeared and progress in learning the piano required more effort and intense involvement, the continuous effect of musical instruction on cognitive development became more dependent upon students' dedication to the task. Perhaps when children start formal music instruction there is an initial improvement in certain cognitive abilities resulting from the new cognitive strategies involved in learning music. However, unless these strategies are further developed through continuous dedication to learning music, the resulting improvements in cognitive abilities might become unnoticeable.

This explanation is in agreement with the results of research comparing the cognitive abilities of musicians and nonmusicians (Barret & Barker, 1973; Hassler et al., 1985; Manturzewska, 1978) and experimental studies conducted with young children (Gromko & Poorman, 1998; Hurwitz et al., 1975; Philbrick & Mallory, 1996, Rauscher, Shaw, et al., 1997). The 6- to 8-month improvement in certain spatial abilities found in children provided with music instruction may have been triggered by the use of newly acquired cognitive strategies, and the superiority of musicians over nonmusicians in certain spatial tests may have been caused by their continuous use of such strategies. At this point, this explanation is speculative because many questions remain unanswered. For example, it is unknown which element of music instruction actually develops these new strategies. In the present study, it could have been the performance of music, the individual attention children received from a caring teacher, the general concentration skills developed during practice, the increased use of symbols that occurred when reading music, or the mere presence of a piano at home. Although traditional piano instruction usually involves all these elements and, as such, contributes to the temporary improvement of certain cognitive abilities, the identification of the exact cause of such improvement could help music educators maximize the beneficial effects of music instruction.

In addition to dedication to learning music, there might be other factors affecting the relationship between music instruction and cognitive development. Hassler and her colleagues (Hassler et al., 1985; Hassler & Nieschlag, 1989; Hassler, 1992), who studied the effects of certain hormones in the development of spatial abilities and creative behavior in music, found that testosterone level is related to artistic talent. This hormone, one of the sex hormones that rises highly during adolescence, was related to the development of spatial abilities in children participating in an 8-year longitudinal study. The relationship between testosterone and spatial abilities was different during their mid-adolescence and late adolescence or adulthood (Hassler, 1992). Interestingly, Hassler found clear differences in spatial abilities between musicians and nonmusicians in adulthood and adolescence, but noticed that these differences were larger during the earlier stages of her longitudinal study than during the later stages. In the present 3-year study, the improvement in spatial abilities was noticed during the first 2 years of treatment when children were between 9 and 12 years old and was not evident after the third year of treatment when children were 12 or 13 years old. It is possible that during the third year of the study when the children were entering preadolescence, hormonal changes had affected their spatial performance or the relationship between music instruction and their spatial development. The absence of data on the children's hormonal changes makes it impossible to study this idea. Future research conducted with children approaching adolescence might consider including measures of hormonal changes when studying the relationship between music and spatial development.

There is a remarkable consistency in the results of this and previous investigations regarding the temporary effects of music instruction on spatial abilities. The differences in the music treatments, spatial abilities measures, and samples used in the various studies did not seem to affect the main conclusion that music treatment can improve certain spatial skills temporarily. While there are contradictions in the literature regarding the specific types of spatial skills affected by music treatments, there seems to be substantial agreement as to the existence of such effects.

In summary, the results of the study showed that the music treatment produced temporary improvements in children's general cognitive abilities and spatial abilities. The 2-year improvement in general and spatial cognitive scores in children might be of interest to educators searching for ways to help children develop their capabilities. Indeed, a period of 2 years represents a considerable length of time in a child's life. However, because in this study the size of the improvements was small and there were no noticeable effects after 3 years of treatment, music educators should be cautious about setting unrealistic expectations regarding the cognitive benefits of music instruction.

References

Barret, H., & Barker, H. (1973). Cognitive pattern perception and musical performance. *Perceptual and Motor Skills, 36*, 1187–1193.

Besson, M., Faita, F., & Requin, J. (1994). Brain waves associated with musical incongruities differ for musicians and non-musicians. *Neuroscience Letters, 168*, 101–105.

Bever, T., & Chiarello, R. (1974). Cerebral dominance in musicians and non-musicians. *Science, 185*, 537–539.

Bruininks-Oseretsky Test of Motor Proficiency. (1978). Circle Pines, MN: American Guidance Center.

Canadian Achievement Tests. (1992). (2nd ed.) Markham, ON: Canadian Test Centre.

Coopersmith Self-Esteem Inventories. (1981). Palo Alto, CA: Consulting Psychologists Press.

Developing Cognitive Abilities Test. (1990). Iowa City, IA: American Testronics.

Duke, B., Flowers, P., & Wolfe, D. (1997). Children who study piano with excellent teachers in the United States. *Bulletin of the Council for Research in Music Education,* no. 132, 51–84.

Gromko, J. E., & Poorman, A. S. (1998). The effect of music training on preschoolers' spatial-temporal task performance. *Journal of Research in Music Education, 46*, 173–181.

Hassler, M. (1992). Creative musical behavior and sex hormones: Musical talent and spatial abilities in the two sexes. *Psychoneouroendocrinology, 17* (1), 55–70.

Hassler, M., Birbaumer, N., & Feil, A. (1985). Musical talent and visual-spatial abilities: A longitudinal study. *Psychology of Music, 13*, 99–113.

Hassler, M., & Nieschlag, E. (1989). Masculinity, femininity, and musical composition: Psychological and psychoendocrinological aspects of musical and spatial faculties. *Archives of Psychology, 141*, 71–84.

Hurwitz, I., Wolff, P., Bortnick, B., & Kokas, K. (1975). Nonmusical effects of the Kodály music curriculum in primary grade children. *Journal of Learning Disabilities, 8* (3), 45–52.

Johnson, J. K., Petsche, H., Richter, P., von Stein, A., & Filz, O. (1996). The dependence of coherence estimates of spontaneous EEG on gender and music training. *Music Perception, 13*, 563–582.

Karma, K. (1979). Musical, spatial and verbal abilities. *Bulletin of the Council for Research in Music Education,* no. 59, 50–53.

Keppel, G. (1982). *Design and analysis: A researcher handbook* (2nd ed.). Englewood Cliffs, NJ: Prentice-Hall Inc.

Manturzewska, M. (1978). Psychology in the music school. *Psychology of Music, 6*, 36–47.

Musical Aptitude Profile. (1988). Chicago, IL: Riverside Publishing Company.

Newman, J., Rosenbach, J., Burns, K., Latimer, B., Matocha, H., Rosenthal, E. (1995). An experimental test of "The Mozart Effect": Does listening to his music improve spatial ability? *Perceptual and Motor Skills, 81*, 1379–1387.

Pilbrick, K., & Mallory, M. (1996, April). *Music and the hemispheres: Stimulating brain development through music education.* Paper presented at the meeting of the Music Educators National Conference, Kansas City, MO.

Rauscher, F., Shaw, G., Levine, L., Ky, K., & Wright, E. (1994, August). *Music and spatial task performance: A causal relationship.* Paper presented at the 102nd Annual Convention of the American Psychological Association, Los Angeles, CA.

Rauscher, F., Robinson, K., & Jens, J. (1997). Spatial performance as a function of early music exposure in rats. In A. Gabrielsson (Ed.), *Proceedings of the European Society for the Cognitive Sciences of Music* (pp. 688–692). Uppsala, Sweden: Uppsala University.

Rauscher, R., Shaw, G., & Ky, N. (1993). Music and spatial task performance. *Nature, 365*, 611.

Rauscher, R., Shaw, G., & Ky, N. (1995). Listening to Mozart enhances spatial-temporal reasoning: Towards a neurophysiological basis. *Neuroscience Letters. 185*, 44.

Rauscher, R., Shaw, G., Levine, L., Wright, E., Dennis, W., & Newcomb, R. (1997). Music training cause long-term enhancement of preschool children's spatial-temporal reasoning. *Neurological Research, 19*, 2.

Rideout, B. E., Dougherty, S., & Wernert, L. (1998). Effect of music on spatial performance: A test of generality. *Perceptual & Motor Skills, 86*, 512–514.

Rideout, B. E, & Taylor, J. (1997). Enhanced spatial performance following 10 minutes' exposure to music: A replication. *Perceptual & Motor Skills, 85*, 112–114.

Sarnthein, J., vonStein, A., Rappelsberger, P., Petsche, H., Rauscher, F., & Shaw, G. (1997). Persistent patterns of brain activity: An EEG coherence study of the positive effect of music on spatial-temporal reasoning. *Neurological Research, 19,* 107–116.

Schlaug, G., Amunts, K., Janke, L., & Zilles, K. (1996). Hand motor covaries with size of motor cortex: Evidence for macrostructural adaptation in musicians. In B. Pennycook & E. Costa-Giomi (Eds), *Proceedings of the International Conference on Music Perception and Cognition* (p. 433). Montreal, QC, Canada.

Schlaug, G., Jancke, L., Hung, Y. & Steinmetz, H. (1995). In vivo evidence of structural brain asymmetry in musicians. *Science, 267,* 699.

Stough, C., Kerkin, B., Bates, T., & Mangan, G. (1994). Music and spatial IQ. *Personality & Individual Differences, 17,* 695.

Eugenia Costa-Giomi is associate professor in the Faculty of Music at McGill University in Montreal, Canada.

Involvement in the Arts and Human Development: General Involvement and Intensive Involvement in Music and Theater Arts

James S. Catterall, Richard Chapleau, and John Iwanaga

This paper was prepared by researchers involved with the UCLA Imagination Project at the Graduate School of Education and Information Studies at the University of California at Los Angeles. This project focuses on arts involvement and its potential ties to academic success in the middle school and high school years.

This report presents results from our work during the past two years exploring interactions between the arts and human development and achievement. This research enlists the National Educational Longitudinal Survey (NELS:88),[1] a panel study which has followed more than 25,000 students in American secondary schools for 10 years. The work addresses developments for children and adolescents over the period spent between the 8th and 12th grades, i.e. late middle school through high school.

The first phase of the work examines involvement in the arts generally—across all disciplines. The second phase examines the potential importance of sustained involvement in a single discipline, here using instrumental music and the theater arts as case examples. We focus on these two arts disciplines because of related research suggesting links between music and cognitive development and between drama and theater in education and various skill and attitude developments.

This chapter is reprinted from James S. Catterall, Richard Chapleau, and John Iwanaga, "Involvement in the Arts and Human Development: General Involvement and Intensive Involvement in Music and Theater Arts," *Champions of Change: The Impact of the Arts on Learning* (Washington, DC: Arts Education Partnership, President's Committee on the Arts & Humanities, GE Fund, and John D. and Catherine T. MacArthur Foundation, 1999). Used with permission.

Our findings, presented in more detail below, can be summarized in three main sets of observations:

(1) *Involvement in the arts and academic success.* Positive academic developments for children engaged in the arts are seen at each step in the research—between 8th and 10th grade as well as between 10th and 12th grade. The comparative gains for arts-involved youngsters generally become more pronounced over time. Moreover and more important, these patterns also hold for children from low socio-economic status (SES) backgrounds.[2]

(2) *Music and mathematics achievement.* Students who report consistent high levels of involvement in instrumental music over the middle and high school years show significantly higher levels of mathematics proficiency by grade 12. This observation holds both generally and for low SES students as a subgroup. In addition, absolute differences in measured mathematics proficiency between students consistently involved versus not involved in instrumental music grow significantly over time.

(3) *Theater arts and human development.* Sustained student involvement in theater arts (acting in plays and musicals, participating in drama clubs, and taking acting lessons) associates with a variety of developments for youth: gains in reading proficiency, gains in self concept and motivation, and higher levels of empathy and tolerance for others. Our analyses of theater arts were undertaken for low SES youth only. Our presumption was that more advantaged youngsters would be more likely to be involved in theater and drama because of attendance at more affluent schools and because of parental ability to afford theater opportunities in the community or private sectors.

We turn first to a brief summary of our initial release of data from this project and then to presentations of some of the important observations from the later research.

I. INITIAL FINDINGS: Involvement in the Arts Generally and Student Academic Outcomes

In mid 1997 we released a report of the effects of involvement in the visual and performing arts on student achievement in middle and high school. Published in the *Americans for the Arts* monograph series as "Involvement in the Arts and Success in Secondary School,"[3] this analysis was based on a multiyear survey of more than 25,000 students sponsored by the United States Department of Education. The sample was created to be representative of the nation's population of secondary students. Our study offered the first reported analysis of information in the NELS:88 survey about student participation in the arts. We used a definition of "involvement in the arts" that gave students credit for taking arts-related classes in or out of school as well as involvement and leadership in school activities such as theater, band, orchestra, chorus, dance, and the visual arts.

Our analyses found substantial and significant differences in achievement and in important attitudes and behaviors between youth highly involved in the arts on the one hand, and those with little or no arts engagement on the other hand. In addition—and more significant from a policy standpoint—the achievement differences between high- and low-arts youth were also significant for economically disadvantaged students. Twenty of the differences we found favoring arts-involved students were significant at the p<.001 level. (This means that the odds of the differences being caused by pure chance were smaller than one in one thousand.) Four differences were significant at the p<.01 level. The only difference not significant was performance on the history geography tests for low SES children.

Figure 1 shows some of the key differences we found between students highly involved in the arts and non-involved students, both for all students in the NELS sample and for the low SES quartile respectively. The figure includes both academic measures and also indicators of students' regard for community service and measures of their television watching habits.

Figure 1 shows consistently more favorable outcomes for students involved in the arts—higher achievement, staying in school, and better attitudes about school and community. We also see marked differences in television watching habits, where arts involved youngsters watch considerably less.

Both our earlier and present efforts provide evidence that achievement differences favoring youngsters involved in the arts are not simply a matter of parent income and education levels, which do tend to line up with children having more visual and performing arts in their lives. Another result, as we spell out in more detail below, is that consistent involvement in the arts shows up in increased advantages for arts-rich

Grade 8 Academic Performance	All Students		Low SES Students	
	High Arts	Low Arts	High Arts	Low Arts
Earning mostly As and Bs in English	79.2%	64.2%	64.5%	56.4%
Scoring in top 2 quartiles on std. tests	66.8%	42.7%	29.5%	24.5%
Dropping out by grade 10	1.4%	4.8%	6.5%	9.4%
Bored in school half or most of the time	42.2%	48.9%	41.0%	46.0%
Grade 10 Academic Performance				
Scoring in top 2 quartiles, Grade 10 Std. Test Composite	72.5%	45.0%	41.4%	24.9%
Scoring in top 2 quartiles in Reading	70.9%	45.1%	43.8%	28.4%
Scoring in top 2 quartiles in History Citizenship, Geography	70.9%	46.3%	41.6%	28.6%
Grade 10 Attitudes and Behaviors				
Consider community service important or very important	46.6%	33.9%	49.2%	40.7%
Television watching, weekdays:				
percentage watching 1 hour or less	28.2%	15.1%	16.4%	13.3%
percentage watching 3 hours or more	20.6%	34.9%	33.6%	42.0%

Figure 1. Comparisons of High Arts vs. Low Arts Students in Grades 8 and 10, All vs Low SES Background

youngsters over time, through 10th grade in our first analyses and through 12th grade in our later studies.

Summarizing Early Results

A case for the importance of the arts in the academic lives of middle and early high schoolers was the primary suggestion of our earlier research. The research did not definitively explain the differences shown, nor was it able to attribute student successes unequivocally to the arts. This caution rises in large part because panel studies are not well suited to unambiguous causal modeling. Nonetheless, the differences were striking, and the chief confounding variable, student family background, was reasonably accounted-for in the work.

There are several theoretical rationales for why the arts might matter in the ways suggested. A previous work by the first author explores much of this ground and points to distinct possibilities.[4] These are grouped into major categories including the various roles that the arts play in promoting cognitive development—from specific relations such as the influence of music on perception and comprehension in mathematics to the more general roles of imagery and representation in cognition. The arts serve to broaden access to meaning by offering ways of thinking and ways of representation consistent with the spectrum of intelligences scattered unevenly across our population—for example, resonating with the multiple and differing intelligences identified by Howard Gardner at Harvard.[5] The arts have also shown links to student motivation and engagement in school, attitudes that contribute to academic achievement.[6] Arts activities also can promote community—advancing shared purpose and team spirit required to perform in an ensemble musical group or dramatic production, or to design and paint an urban mural. With community surely comes empathy and general attachment to the larger values of the school and the adult society which high school students will soon join.

Readers will note that we do not address here anything having to do with achievement in the arts per se, itself an important domain apart from any connections between the arts and more traditional academic success. The NELS: 88 data base shows a marked absence of indicators of achievement in the arts—a problem that should not go unnoticed as future national longitudinal surveys are planned.

Finally, even in the absence of causal attributions yet to be proved, the perspectives we show elicit another reason to promote more involvement in the arts for more youngsters. This is the likely positive peer associations accompanying involvement in the arts. Our analysis of the NELS:88 survey established, for the first time in any comprehensive way, that students involved in the arts are doing better in school than those who are not—for whatever constellation of reasons. Compendia of research on academic achievement going back three decades and more argue that the motivation and success of one's peers has an influence on how a youngster does in school. At very least, even our early comparisons support the contention that rubbing shoulders with arts-involved youngsters in the middle and high school years is typically a smart idea when it comes to choosing friends and activities.

More Recent Findings

Grants to the Imagination Project at UCLA from the GE Fund in September of 1997 and December of 1998 supported extensions of this research. There were three general priorities for the newly-funded work:

One priority was to extend the analyses describing developments up to grade 10 through the balance of high school and beyond. We here report results through grade 12.

A second priority was to begin to conceptualize involvement in the arts in ways that could capture the potential value of "depth" of involvement. Our earlier work relied on measures of involvement that tended to reward widespread involvement over many artistic pursuits; the most "involved" students in our first study were largely those who attached themselves vigorously to several disciplines. There are good reasons, however, to believe that intensive involvement in a single discipline would act differently than scattered attention to diverse artistic endeavors. This is because different effects are touted for different arts disciplines, and depth of involvement in one might be expected to intensify particular effects.

A third priority for the research was to explore possible connections between involvement in music and cognitive development. Much interest has been generated by recent studies in neuroscience linking certain types of music training with positive developments in cognitive functioning. (We refer here especially to various studies of Gordon Shaw, Frances Rauscher, and others over the past 6 years described below.)

Our first effort to explore the impact of depth of experience in the arts focused on students who reported sustained involvement in instrumental music, blending priorities two and three. Our second effort was to examine students who reported sustained involvement in theater arts. The theoretical rationales for inquiry aimed at theater derive largely from a literature focused on theater in education and drama in the classroom produced mainly over several decades of research and scholarly writing in Great Britain.

Extending Analyses of Effects of Involvement in the Arts through Grade 12

Before examining outcomes, we first found that levels of student involvement in the arts declined between grades 10 and 12. As of the spring of the senior year, twelfth graders fell off in reported involvement in the arts when compared to grade 10. For example, whereas 22.7 percent of 10th graders reported involvement in band or orchestra and 23.3 percent showed involvement in chorus or choir, fewer than 20 percent showed involvement in any school musical group by grade 12, as shown in Figure 2. Figure 2 also shows that the percentages of students taking out-of-school classes in music, art, or dance also declined markedly between grades 10 and 12. Especially notable is the drop from more than 11 percent to fewer than 3 percent of students taking daily out of school lessons in grade 10 versus grade 12.

Grade 12			Grade 10		
Participates in:	School Music Group	19.5%	Band or Orchestra	22.7%	
	School Play/Musical	15.0	Chorus or Choir	23.3%	
Takes out-of-school classes in Music, Art, or Dance:			Takes out-of-school classes in Music, Art, or Dance:		
rarely or never		85.9%	rarely or never:	74.2%	
less than 1/week		4.2	less than 1/week	5.8	
1-2 per week		7.4	1-2 per week	8.6	
every day or almost		2.5	every day or almost	11.3	

Figure 2. Percentages of Students Involved in Arts Related Activities Reported in the NELS:88 Data Base, Grade 12 vs. Grade 10.

High- Versus Low-Arts Involvement and General Student Performance

One of our objectives in the latest phase of this research was to extend earlier analyses through grade 12. In Figure 3, we recount key observed differences between high- and low-arts involved students as of grades 8 and 10, and then show differences accruing through grade 12.

As seen in Figure 3, performance differences between arts-involved and non-involved students remained about the same across grade levels in nominal terms—showing up typically as 16 to 18 percentage point differences. For example, the percentage of low-arts students scoring in the top half of the standardized test distribution was 47.5 percent in grade 10, while 65.7 percent of high-arts students scored above the test score median—an 18.2 percentage point difference at that grade level. At grade 12, the respective figures are 39.3 and 57.4 percent, an 18.1 percentage point difference.

Within the general trends in achievement differences, it can be seen that the relative advantage of involvement in the arts increased appreciably over time. This is shown in the relative sizes of the sub-groups doing well from the arts-involved and non-involved groups respectively, which grow over time. By the 12th grade, the nominal 18 percentage point difference amounts to a 46 percent advantage for the high-arts group where 57.4 percent scored well compared to 39.3 percent from the low-arts group (57.4/39.3 = 1.46 or a 46 percent advantage.)

8th Grade

% in each group	High Involvement	Low Involvement
Earning mostly As and Bs in English	82.6%	67.2%
Top 2 quartiles on std. tests	67.3%	49.6%
Dropping out by grade 10	1.4%	3.7%
Bored in school half or most of time	37.9%	45.9%

10th Grade

% in each group	High Involvement	Low Involvement
Top 2 quartiles std. tests	65.7%	47.5%
Top 2 quartiles Reading	64.7%	45.4%
Level 2 (high) Reading Proficiency	61.0%	43.5%
Top 2 quartiles History/Geography/ Citizenship	62.9%	47.4%

12th Grade

% in each group	High Involvement	Low Involvement
Top 2 quartiles std tests	57.4%	39.3%
Top 2 quartiles Reading	56.5%	37.7%
Level 2 or 3 (high) Reading Proficiency	58.8%	42.9%
Top 2 quartiles History/Geography/ Citizenship	54.6%	39.7

Figure 3. Involvement in the Arts and Academic Performance

Figure 4 shows what the comparative achievement advantages for involvement in the arts look like over time for all students; all group differences (except the history/geography test for low SES students) are significant at greater than a 99 percent confidence level. Most remain significant at the .999 confidence level.

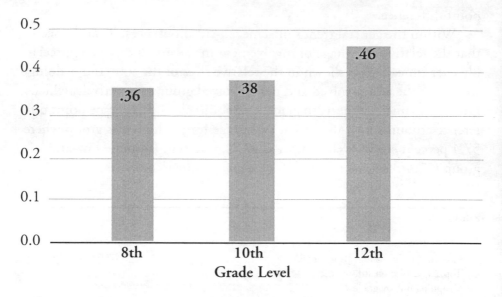

Figure 4. Comparative Advantages in Composite Test Scores, High vs. Low Arts, Grades 8 through 12

This general pattern of increasing advantage is replicated for various measures in addition to composite test scores—meaning that high arts youngsters did comparatively better on multiple measures as they passed from grade 8 to grade 12.

Socio-Economic Status and Involvement in the Arts

As shown in Figure 5 below, we continue to find substantial differences in the family income and education levels between our high arts

Probability of High Arts Involvement	
High SES Quartile	.320
Low SES Quartile	.178
Probability of Low Arts Involvement	
High SES Quartile	.197
Low SES Quartile	.385

Figure 5. Probability of High vs. Low Arts Involvement by Student SES

and low arts groups. The probability of being "high arts" remains almost twice as high for students from economically advantaged families, and the probablility of low arts involvement is about twice as high if one comes from an economically disadvantaged family.

This is why the following analyses of achievement restricted to low SES students are very important. Not only are achievement issues typically more profound for children from families with less education and fewer economic resources, but high SES children simply have more opportunities to be involved in the arts. When we compare groups of students by arts involvement only, the differences are more likely to be caused by differences in family background than anything else.

Achievement Differences, Low SES Students

Here we begin with our findings concerning grade 8, grade 10, and grade 12 performance differences within the low SES quartile—the fourth of all students at the bottom of the family income and education ladder. This group represents families where parents typically graduated from high school and went no further with their education, as well as families where parents never finished high school.

As shown in Figure 6, the patterns shown for low SES students over time bear similarities to those shown for all students. The percentage differences in performance are smaller in nominal terms—for example 8 to 10 percent lower for test scores. But once again, the relative advantage for arts-involved youngsters increases over the middle and high school years, and especially between grades 10 and 12.

Figure 7 illustrates this pattern for composite standardized test scores where the comparative advantage for high arts, low-SES youngsters is about 32 percent by grade 12.

This concludes our presentation concerning differences between students generally highly involved in the arts as compared to their non-involved peers. The main points of the analysis so far are that arts involved students do better on many measures, their performance advantages grow over time, and that these two general performance comparisons also hold for low SES children. We will probe these findings in more detail in the discussion concluding this monograph. We turn now to two cases of intensive involvement in specific arts disciplines.

% in each group	High Involvement	Low Involvement
Top 2 quartiles std tests	37.7%	29.8%
Mostly As and Bs in English	71.4%	58.8%
Dropping out by grade 10	3.5%	6.5%
Bored in school half or most of time	32.9%	40.1%

10th Grade

% in each group	High Involvement	Low Involvement
Top 2 quartiles std tests	35.2%	28.1%
Top 2 quartiles reading	37.3%	28.7%
Level 2 Reading Proficiency	39.6%	29.2%
Top 2 quartiles History/Geography/ Citizenship	34.8%	30.4%

12th Grade

% in each group	High Involvement	Low Involvement
Top 2 quartiles std tests	30.9%	23.4%
Top 2 quartiles reading	32.9%	23.6%
Top 2 quartiles History/Geography/ Citizenship	30.7%	25.2%
Level 2 or 3 Reading Proficiency	37.9%	30.4%

Figure 6. Involvement in the Arts and Academic Performance and Attitudes, Low SES Students (Low Parent Education/Income)

II. INTENSIVE INVOLVEMENT WITHIN AN ARTS DISCIPLINE: The Cases of Instrumental Music and Drama/Theater

A new strain of our work, and a departure from our first monograph which adopted a more general orientation to involvement in the arts, is a study of youngsters who exhibit very high levels of involvement within a single arts discipline over the secondary school years. Readers may recall that the analyses reported above were built on a conception of involvement defined as "the more involvement in more arts, the higher the student's involvement score." As such, a student who only participated in an orchestra and took music lessons, no matter how intensively, would not have been a high-arts student in our first analyses.

Yet intensive involvement in a single discipline should probably be thought to be even more important developmentally than high levels of more diverse involvement in the arts. This is surely true if specific arts act

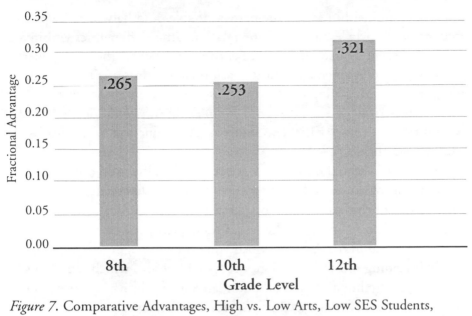

Figure 7. Comparative Advantages, High vs. Low Arts, Low SES Students, Grades 8–12, Standardized Test Scores

in specific ways on cognition or other developments. That is an assumption we are comfortable making and could defend at some length. In general, the argument is that different art forms involve different skills and different sorts of human interaction. In short, they impact cognitive and motor processes differently and should be expected to result in different outcomes. We will save a more in-depth discussion of this for another paper.

Involvement in Instrumental Music

Involvement in Instrumental Music and Cognitive Development in Mathematics. We were interested in exploring involvement in music because of accumulated studies over the past 7-8 years suggesting that certain kinds of musical experiences, especially keyboard training, seem to produce effects on cognitive functioning in young children. Other potentially important aspects of the musical experience are learning to read music and to associate musical notation with abstract concepts of time, rhythm, and pitch. These experiences at first glance appear to involve forms of mathematical reasoning—the fractional senses of different musical notes (whole notes, half notes, and so on), the relative distances of notes within scales, the perfect doubles and halves in the pitch frequencies of octaves, and even the relations among dynamics within a musical passage. For some musical instruments, such as the piano, there is an associated geometry of music that probably reinforces the spatial-temporal reasoning effects noted by Rauscher et al. For other instruments, such as the strings, there are complex linear geometries associated with pitch that bring spatial reasoning to the production of musical sounds and phrases.

What has research on music suggested? While it would appear that the domains of music and mathematics are widely divergent, an increasing number of studies focusing on participation in musical activity and cognitive development in mathematics suggest that the two are closely related. An important skill developed while a child begins the study of music is reading musical notation, the symbol system which represents elements of rhythm and pitch, the fundamental building blocks of music. It is the analysis of music at this basic level which reveals the most obvious connection between music and mathematics (Bahna-James, 1991).

Rhythm, here defined as a numerical pattern of beats occurring over time, is represented by a series of notes ranging from whole notes (usually 1 beat per measure) to quarter notes (4 beats per measure) to eighth, sixteenth and even 32nd and 64th notes. Two fundamental mathematical skills are required in order to understand the time meaning represented in a note: the ability to count beats, which allows for an understanding of the absolute value of a note in a measure, and general fractional or proportional sense, which allows for an understanding of each note type in relation to the other.

A second feature depicted by musical notation is pitch or frequency, which denotes the relative tonal distances between notes within scales, chords, and intervals. These relationships in and of themselves are abstract and difficult to conceptualize; the use of musical instruments such as the violin, clarinet, or piano helps make these tonal relationships concrete. The keyboard in particular has been singled out in research by Rauscher and Shaw (1997) on spatial-temporal reasoning as a form of reasoning ability postulated to directly affect mathematical understanding. The results from their work show that keyboard training is a more effective intervention on spatial-temporal reasoning skills than singing lessons and computer training and suggest that mastering a musical instrument aids in developing mathematical understanding.

Initial studies correlating the grades of secondary school students in music theory and math classes (Bahna-James, 1991) as well as teacher evaluation of instrumental and scholastic achievement for elementary school students (Klinedinst, 1991) revealed a variety of significant relationships between mathematics achievement and music performance. These included sightsinging and arithmetic, algebra and geometry; pitch and arithmetic; and finally tonal relationships and arithmetic and algebra. The work by Bahna-James (1991) further showed that the correlation between math grades and music theory grades of secondary school students increases when the mathematics being taught is of a more elementary level and the numerical relationships are simple. Some findings provide additional support for the notion that the fundamental components of music are inherently mathematical in nature.

Research by Shaw et al. (Boettcher, Hahn & Shaw, 1994; Grandin, Peterson & Shaw, 1998; Graziano, Shaw & Wright, 1997; Rauscher & Shaw, 1997; Rauscher & Shaw, 1998) drawing in part from the seminal work of Chase & Simon (1973) on how chess experts process information, has suggested that cognition in music, mathematics and complex games are activities driven by pattern recognition and manipulation, and as such are affected by spatial-temporal reasoning ability. Of particular interest is their study (mentioned above) which focuses on the effect of keyboard training on the spatial-temporal reasoning of young children as measured by a series of object assembly tasks. These assembly tasks require matching, classifying, and recognizing similarities and relationships among displayed objects. Keyboard training alone (rather than training in singing or simple arithmetic through the use of computer games) had a significant effect on children's ability to classify and recognize similarities and relationships between objects; this provides further evidence for the contention that at the most abstract level, music, like mathematics, requires the ability to recognize patterns and relations.

Intensive Music Involvement in NELS:88. We here report our explorations of differences shown by students who were heavily involved in instrumental music throughout the first three panels of the NELS:88 survey—8th, 10th and 12th grades. We add a word of caution at this point. Some of the studies discussed above were studies of music experiences in their natural state and their associations with spatial-temporal reasoning or mathematics-related learning. These were generally situations where there was no intention in the curriculum to bolster math-related skills;

the researchers simply wondered if increased skills related to mathematics were a serendipitous byproduct of the music experience. Other studies were launched with the expressed intention of producing and tracking connections between learning in both the musical and mathematical domains. Both types of studies have found connections between music and mathematics cognition. Our work focuses on apparently serendipitous associations between reported involvement in instrumental music and reports of growth in mathematics proficiency for students.

The following chart shows one early result of our work. We examined the probability that students in different groups—differing mainly by involvement in instrumental music—would attain the highest levels of mathematics proficiency on the 12th grade tests used in the NELS:88 study. We also differentiated our analyses by family income and education levels, or SES.

In Figure 8 below, it can be seen that the overall probability of scoring high in mathematics (that is, the probability of such performance among all 12th grade students) is about 21 percent. These students score at Levels 4 and 5 on the NELS:88 mathematics test, performance levels indicative of strong success through at least three years of high school mathematics. From this baseline, the comparisons become quite interesting. First, all high SES students in our "high" and "no music" groups do better in mathematics than the average student. Second, within groups, students concentrating in instrumental music do substantially better in

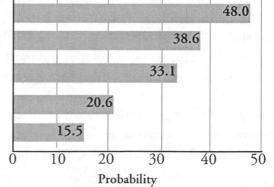

Figure 8. Probability of Highest Math Proficiency (Levels 4 or 5), Grade 12, By Group—SES and Consistent High vs. No Involvement in Band/Orchestra

mathematics than those with no involvement in music. And third, low SES students with high involvement in music do better than the average student at attaining high levels of mathematics proficiency. The performance distribution for extremely low levels of mathematics proficiency, Level 1 and below, is a mirror opposite to the one shown in Figure 8.

Do math skills grow over time with involvement in instrumental music?

The NELS:88 data base allows for comparisons over time, an important feature in the creation of arguments addressing the causes of observed differences between or among groups of interest. Here we observe how music-involved students compared with their non-music peers as of 8th grade and revisit the exact same students again in grade 12. Figure 9 shows performance level distributions for grade 8 groups of interest, including overall average scores, averages for all low SES students, averages of all low SES students with no music involvement, and low SES students with high involvement in orchestra and/or band. The

Math Proficiency Scores v	Average N=14,915	Average— Low SES N=7,052	No Music— Low SES N=1,216	Orch/Band— Low SES N=260
Below 1	15.3	20.8	16.4	10.8
Level 1	34.7	41.1	42.1	36.9
Level 2	20.3	17.8	19.7	20.4
Level 3	19.0	8.6	10.7	21.2

Figure 9. Math Proficiency Scores at Grade 8, Percentages Scoring at Each Level

levels shown refer to successively higher levels of proficiency, and they are scaled by specific skills and knowledge of test takers. (The NELS:88 test used here are criterion-referenced exams, like the tests used for the National Assessment of Educational Progress.) Their purpose is to gauge skill development against standards of performance and not to place students on some national norm scale. Level 3 would be considered high-performing at grade 8; Levels 4 and 5 would be considered high-performing at grade 12.)

In Figure 9, it can be seen that twice as many low SES 8th graders in Band and/or Orchestra score at high levels in mathematics as did low SES 8th graders with no reported involvement in instrumental music—

Math Proficiency Scores	Average	Average— Low SES	No Music— Low SES	Orch/Band— Low SES
v	N=14,915	N=7,052	N=1,216	N=260
Below 1	4.7	6.4	5.3	1.9
Level 1	14.8	20.9	22.8	12.7
Level 2	8.9	10.5	13.1	13.5
Level 3	15.6	14.6	21.1	20.8
Level 4	18.3	10.9	14.5	30.4
Level 5	3.0	.9	1.0	2.7

Figure 10. Math Proficiency Scores at Grade 12, Percentages Scoring at Each Level

21.2 percent versus only 10.7 percent. For grade 8, the percentages of low SES students who would eventually show consistently high involvement in orchestra/band show math scores lower the average student, with about 10.8 percent of music-involved students scoring very low (below Level 1) and 15.3 percent of all students scoring as poorly. By grade 12, the differentials increasingly favor students heavily involved in instrumental music, especially the percentages of students performing at the highest levels (levels 4 and 5).

Through summing percentages shown in Figure 10 for students performing at levels 4 and 5, we see that thirty-three percent of high-music/low SES students test at high levels of mathematics proficiency. This 33.1 percent should be compared to only 21.3 percent for "all" students, and only 15.5 percent of no-music, low SES students who score at high levels in mathematics by grade 12.

A most significant dynamic underlies the data in Figure 10. As of 8th grade, low SES, high-music youngsters perform on a par with the average student—about 21 percent at high math proficiency versus 19 percent for the average student. By 12th grade, the high performing gap between low SES, high-music students and the average student has grown to about 33 percent versus 21 percent.

Figure 11 shows how the absolute performance gaps between the low SES students involved in music versus low SES non-music youth have grown considerably between grades 8 and 12.

Figure 11 shows math proficiency developments for low SES youngsters in perspective. In the NELS sample, there were 260 low SES students who qualified as intensively involved in instrumental music over

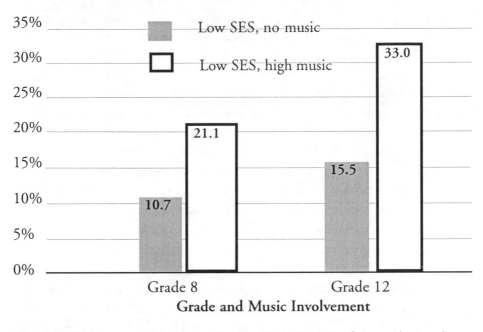

Figure 11. Percentages of Students Scoring High Math Proficiency, by involve-ment level in instrumental music, Low SES

the span of grades 8 through 12. As of the 8th grade, these 260 students were outperforming the 1,216 low SES students with no music involve-ment in mathematics; about 20 versus 10 percent scored at the highest lev-els of the mathematics proficiency scale. By grade 12, these same 260 stu-dents were outperforming all low SES no-music students by a considerably larger margin—about 33 percent were at the highest levels of mathematics performance versus only 15 percent for their non-music peers.

Involvement in Theater

We turn here to another exploration of intensive involvement in a single artistic discipline, in this case the theater arts.

Our interest in the theater arts grows from a history of scholarship exploring the meaning and importance of theater and drama in educa-tion over the past three decades. The central figures are a number of prominent university faculty in Great Britain. The United Kingdom has been the setting for a substantial Theater in Education (or TIE) movement during this time.[7] TIE refers to theatrical companies taking up residencies of varying duration at schools, usually bringing productions designed to provoke thought and discussion of important themes, as well as to entertain. There are also numerous devotees of "drama in education" in England, including many of the nation's elementary school teachers. This term refers to the use of drama in the classroom for various purposes—learning about history, conflict resolution, learning about oneself, learning stagecraft, learning acting, and so on.[8] Drama in education is formally recognized as a curricular tool in the current National Curriculum in Britain, although neither drama nor theater are required subjects. University teacher education faculties maintain lectureships and even a professorship or two in drama in education, so that teachers in training can learn to use dramatic forms in their future classrooms. Britain also boasts a remarkable individual, Dorothy Heathcote, who has become a legendary teacher trainer through a non-stop series of teacher workshops and residencies that have not slowed for 40 years, even as she enters her mid-70s. Ms. Heathcote advocates that teachers get into roles, along with their students, as they teach. She usually presents her workshops in role to make her points.

In surveying what is known about the impact of theater and drama on children, Tony Jackson from the University of Manchester identifies "change of understanding" as the general purpose. He goes on to emphasize that the changes of understanding can be about both form and content in theater. Children learn about the art form as well as about other ends related to personal or social development. Among the latter, Jackson enumerates learning about "group interaction, discipline, language usage, self esteem and movement skills."[9] Heathcote reminds us also that drama provides situations where we can or must put ourselves into the place of another; thus empathy for others is a possible or even likely outcome of the dramatic experience.[10]

The strength of evidence for specific impacts of theater and drama claimed by these and other scholars tends to be weak. Drama and theater are complex events with many possible effects. Even if it were feasible to design studies looking for the impact of theater experience on such things as actor self esteem or language facility, objections by artists about taking so narrow a view of the experience would likely interfere. In any event, what we tend most to benefit from is the accumulation of case studies,[11] and the informed observations of senior scholars who have been attached to TIE or drama in education and who have come to their own understanding through the gradual acquisition of research and professional knowledge.

We turn in a moment to our exploration of developments for middle and high-schoolers intensively involved in theater and drama. But we should begin by noting that the theater in education experiences on which we focus are not strictly those of central interest to scholars of drama and theater in education in the UK. The students in our study identified through NELS:88 data as intensively involved in theater are those who have attended a drama class once per week or more as of 8th grade, participated in a drama club as of 8th grade, taken drama coursework in grade 10, and participated in a school play or musical in grades 10 and 12—or at least most of the above. Officers of these organizations were assigned extra "credit" toward intense involvement.

As such, our drama and theater students were not necessarily associated with TIE (formal theater groups in residence on campus) or with drama in education (the use of dramatic forms in the individual classroom for various curricular purposes). These are the kingpins of drama and theater in education in Britain and the experiences generating our hypotheses for this exploration. Our interest centered on whether or not some of the claimed benefits of drama and theater from across the Atlantic show up in the NELS:88 data.

Theater and Language Skills. NELS:88 does not contain a measure of spoken language skills, but the data do track the development of reading proficiency over each survey year. We examined the progression of reading skills for two groups of low SES students beginning in grade 8. One group had no involvement in theater, and the other group was highly involved in theater. (This group consisted of the 285 highest theater-involved, low SES students in the entire NELS:88 sample.)

The pattern in the reading proficiency data is fairly clear. The involved students outscored the noninvolved students as of 8th grade; both groups gain skill as they proceed through high school; and the difference favoring students involved in theater grows steadily to where nearly 20 percent more are reading at high proficiency by grade 12. (The advantage was only 9 percent back in grade 8.) This seems reasonable in that students involved in drama and theater, according to our definition of intensive involvement, probably spend time reading and learning lines as actors, and possibly reading to carry out research on characters and

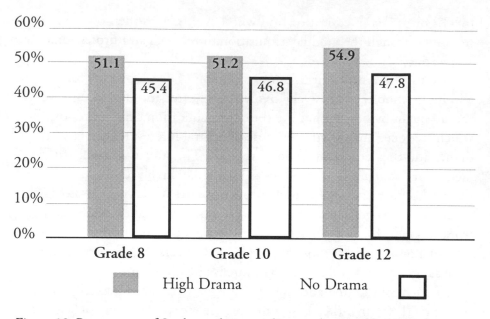

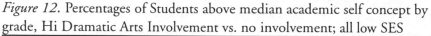

Figure 12. Percentages of Students above median academic self concept by grade, Hi Dramatic Arts Involvement vs. no involvement; all low SES

their settings. In any case, theater is a language rich environment and actively engages students with issues of language.

Theater and Self Concept. Because the English researchers list self esteem as a corollary of engagement with drama and theater, we examined the progression of a general self-concept measure in NELS:88 over grades 8 through 12 and compared our theater-involved to non-involved low SES students. Figure 12 shows that the "high drama" group maintained a small edge in self concept throughout the longitudinal study. Both groups gain over the four years involved, and a slightly bigger gap favoring those intensively involved in theater opened up by grade 12. (By grade 12, the difference shown in Figure 12 became significant (p<.058)).

Involvement in Theater and Empathy and Tolerance. Dorothy Heathcote reminded us that a dramatic experience is an opportunity to put oneself into another's shoes. This is true when taking on a role; it is also true when, as a character in role, one labors to understand how another character encountered on stage has conceptualized and enacted his or her role, or to comprehend how his or her character is understood by others. Theater is loaded with potential opportunities to interact with students to whom one might not gravitate in the ordinary course of school life, including students from other economic strata and other racial groups. This holds both for interactions in role and for interactions with other members of the cast as a play or scene or improvisation is developed.

We found two indicators related to "tolerance" and "empathy" in NELS:88 and show the results on the following pages. Once again, we are comparing low SES students, one group with no involvement in theater and the other with high involvement over all of the high school years.

Race Relations. The first indicator is shown in Figure 13. This reflects student responses to the question, "Are students friendly with other racial groups?" Students involved in theater are more likely than all 12th graders to say yes to this question, by 27 percent to 20 percent. This difference may be an effect of involvement in theater. It also may be an artifact of unknown differences in schools attended by students where theater programs are offered. For other unknown reasons, relations among racial groups may be more positive at the schools of our high-theater involvement students. This difference is not statistically significant, in part an artifact of the small low-SES, high-theater sample.

A similar perspective is shown in Figure 14 on the following page. Here students at grade 10 were asked if it was OK, where only about 12

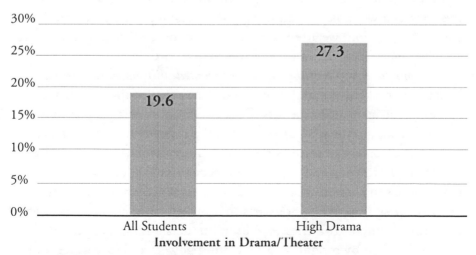

Figure 13. Are students friendly with other racial groups? Students in lowest 2 SES quartiles.

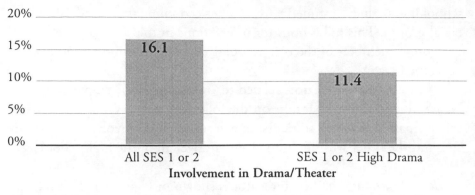

Figure 14. Percentage of 10th Graders who feel it's OK to make Racist Remarks

percent of high theater students thought the same, and about 17 percent of no theater students agreed. In this case, the advantage favoring high-theater students is statistically significant (p<.05).

As with the data bearing on students "getting along" with others of different races (Figure 13), what is shown in Figure 14 may indicate an effect of involvement in theater and it may also be influenced by unknown school differences.

Discussion

The kinds of comparisons and analyses shown above are sure to provoke several kinds of questions surrounding the meaning of the data and the approach we took to examining and displaying the figures. In this concluding section, we attempt to anticipate some of these questions and also to suggest the implications of what we report.

Are our conceptions of the arts too concerned with non-arts outcomes? The purpose of this research was to examine some of the non-arts outcomes of engagement in the arts. Because we chose this purpose does not mean that we do not recognize or value the myriad goals that education in and involvement in the arts serve. Certainly involvement in the broad spectrum of arts captured in our more general assessment will mean many things to students that we did not set out to capture. Not the least of these are skills in the various arts themselves, competencies as critics of art forms, aesthetic awarenesses, cultural understandings, appreciations valuable in their own right, and newfound powers and joys to see and express.

Our analysis of involvement in instrumental music captured a sense of this activity that is clearly not an intentional part of music instruction or participation for many. It just happens that research is suggesting links between music and mathematics reasoning that we took the opportunity to explore. A larger case for instrumentality connected to theater and drama has been articulated in the writings and research of English scholars, and we explored a handful of such possibilities through NELS:88 data.

So yes, this analysis is concerned with non-arts outcomes of the arts in education. For now, we save research on the arts-related goals of arts education and participation in the arts for other scholars and to us, for a future date.

What can be said about causation in this analysis? Establishing causation in education and social science research is difficult. The essential question that should be aimed at this type of work is what evidence supports contentions that involvement in the arts, or music, or theater "caused" the differences in groups reported above.

Any convictions that causation is involved depend mainly on three elements of the research—sound theory, supportive evidence, and ruling out rival explanations. First is the presence of a sound theory consistent with explanations that the arts should matter. In the case of all three of our analyses, we built our instincts around previous research suggestive of causal propositions. The strength of the case is perhaps most developed in the instance of music and mathematics-related cognitive development. Incidental benefits of theater have been argued and studied in the UK for decades. The general effects of broad involvement in the arts are supported most by research that has shown that children are more engaged and cognitively involved in school when the arts are part of, or integrated into, the curriculum.[12]

A second element is observational data supporting the causal theory. If one cannot find an empirical link between participation in the arts and specific outcomes, it is difficult to argue that the arts are causing anything. A version of this argument is that one cannot support causation without significant correlation. The tables above illustrate correlations between arts participation and various outcomes, some quite strong.

The third element is the elimination of rival hypotheses. This is first carried out by trying to make comparison groups as similar as possible, with the only remaining difference being, in our case, intensive arts participation or none. We pursued this by restricting our groups to low SES students, so that differences in family background would not be driving observed differences. We also tend to eliminate rival hypotheses by observing changes over time for the same students. In all three sections of the work, advantages favoring arts—involved students appear to grow over time, which strengthens the sense of causal ordering—first arts immersion, then developmental effects.

A rival hypothesis we have not ruled out is that, systematically, the more arts-involved students attended more effective schools over middle and high school. To be truly preemptive, a "better school" explanation would have to hold for all three of our main comparison frames (general arts involvement, music involvement, and theater involvement). These comparisons were constructed differently, showed arts advantage on many different outcomes, and involved different students and different schools. An overriding better school explanation is not likely.

What are the implications of this research? This paper presents observations from a large-scale data base of U.S. secondary school students suggesting positive associations between involvement in various arts and academic and social outcomes. The work supports strong suggestions, but is not definitive. No one study ever decides issues in this sort of research. Our knowledge base grows incrementally with the accumulation of consistent studies, and with the accumulation of professional knowledge by educators, school leaders, parents, students, and in this case artists involved in the schools.

The main implication of this work is that the arts appear to matter when it comes to a variety of non-arts outcomes, some of them intended and some not. The advantages accruing to arts involvement show up as both a general relationship, as well as in relations between specific developments for youngsters.

In addition, although not the main theme of this paper, our data support long-held concerns that access to the arts is inequitably distributed in our society. Students from poor and less educated families are much more likely to record low levels of participation in the arts during the middle and high school years; affluent youngsters are much more likely to show high, rather than low engagement in the arts. If our analysis is reasonable, the arts do matter—not only as worthwhile experiences in their own right for reasons not addressed here, but also as instruments of cognitive growth and development and as agents of motivation for school success. In this light, unfair access to the arts for our children brings consequences of major importance to our society.

Finally, this work also suggests the value of future research. One important stream would be to follow the NELS:88 sample into young adulthood to explore sustaining effects. Another is the promise of more up-close and controlled research that could further test our findings. Traditionally, the strongest research approach is the use of randomized studies. But random assignment to involvement in the arts is problematic when the issue is long term, natural engagement with the arts—the topic our research is concerned with. Also, long term deprivation in the arts, implied when enlisting purposeful control groups to study the importance of the arts, is probably unethical and could be considered potentially harmful to children.

Productive approaches to additional research may include phenomenological studies that probe the meanings of art experiences to individual children or educators. Studies may include up-close longitudinal studies of students heavily involved in music or theater (or other art disciplines) at the single or multiple-school level to explore changes over time. Studies should include school-level or larger scale studies of initiatives attempting to bring arts integration to the curriculum.[13] Knowledge will grow at the intersection of multiple and diverse studies of what the arts mean for human development.

Notes

1. NELS:88 is managed by the National Center for Education Statistics at the Office for Educational Research and Improvement, United States Department of Education. The data and code books are available in various forms on CD Rom media for public use.

2. SES, or socioeconomic status, is a measure of family education level, income, and type of job(s) held by parents.

3. James S. Catterall, *Involvement in the Arts and Success in Secondary School.* Washington, DC: Americans for the Arts monograph series, No. 9, 1998.

4. See Jaye T. Darby and James S. Catterall. The fourth R: The arts and learning. *Teachers College Record* (1995).

5. See Howard Gardner: *Frames of Mind* (New York: Basic Books), 1983; and *The Arts and Human Development* (New York: John Wiley), 1973.

6. See Morrison Institute of Public Policy and The National Endowment for the Arts, *Schools, Communities, and the Arts: A Research Compendium.*

Tempe, AZ: The Morrison Institute for Public Policy, Arizona State University and the National Endowment for the Arts (1995). Especially summary of report on the National Longitudinal Study of Different Ways of Knowing (The Galef Institute, Los Angeles). See also the monograph reporting evaluations of the Chicago Arts Partnerships in Education, this volume.

7. See Tony Jackson, *Learning Through Theater: New perspectives on theater in education.* Second edition. London:Routlege, 1993.

8. See Gavin Bolton, *Drama as Education: An argument for placing drama at the center of the curriculum.* Longman, 1984.

9. Jackson, op. cit, p. 44.

10. O'Neill and Johnson, op.cit. p. 129.

11. Tony Jackson. *Learning Through Theater: Essays and Casebooks on Theater in Education.* Manchester: Manchester University, 1980. Also Dorothy Heathcote, *Drama and Learning*, Chapter in O'Neil and Johnson, op.cit. pp. 90-102.

12. See chapter in *Champions of Change* on the evaluation of the Chicago Arts Partnerships in Education for discussions and evidence concerning integration of the arts into the academic curriculum.

13. The Imagination Project is currently conducting such an investigation—the 6th and 7th year evaluations of the Chicago Arts Partnerships in Education. See summary report in *Champions of Change.*

References

Bahna-James, T. (1991). The relationship between mathematics and music: secondary school student perspectives. *Journal of Negro Education, 60,* 477-485.

Boettcher, W., Hahn, S., & Shaw, G. (1994). Mathematics and music: A search for insight into higher brain function. *Leonardo Music Journal, 4,* 53-58.

Bolton, G., (1984) *Drama as Education: An argument for placing drama at the center of the curriculum.* Longman.

Chase, W.G. & Simon, H.A. (1973). Perception in Chess. *Cognitive Psychology, 4,* 55-81.

Darby, J. T. & Catterall, J.S. (1994). The fourth R: The arts and learning. *Teachers College Record, 96/2.*

Grandin, T., Peterson, M., & Shaw, G. (1998). Spatial-temporal versus language analytic reasoning: The role of music training. *Arts Education Policy Review, 99,* 11-14.

Graziano, A., Shaw, G., & Wright, E. (1997). Music training enhances spatial-temporal reasoning in young children. *Early Childhood Connections,* Summer, 31-37.

Heathcote, D.(1984) *Drama and Learning,* Chapter in O'Neill and Johnson, op.cit. pp. 90-102.

Jackson, T. (1980) *Learning Through Theater: Essays and Casebooks on Theater in Education.* Manchester: Manchester University.

Jackson, T. (1993) *Learning Through Theater: new perspectives on theater in education.* Second edition. London: Routledge.

Klinedinst, R. (1991). Predicting performance achievement and retention of fifth-grade instrumental students. *Journal of Research in Music Education,* 39, 225-238.

O'Neill, C. and Johnson, L. (1984) *Dorothy Heathcote: Collected Writings on Education and Drama.* Cheltenham, UK: Stanley Thornes (Publishers) Ltd.

Rauscher, E, Shaw, G., & Ky, K. (1995). Listening to Mozart enhances spatial-temporal reasoning: towards a neurophysiological basis. *Neuroscience Letters,* 185, 44-47.

Rauscher, F., Shaw G., Levine, L., Wright, E., Dennis W., & Newcomb, R. (1997). Music training causes long-term enhancement of preschool children's spatial-temporal reasoning. *Neurological Research,* 19, 2-8.

Rauscher, F., & Shaw, G. (1998). Key components of the Mozart effect. *Perceptual and Motor Skills,* 86, 835-841.

The Intrinsic
Value of
Music Education

Growing Up Complete: The Imperative for Music Education

The National Commission on Music Education

The National Commission on Music Education was formed in 1990 under the sponsorship of MENC, NAMM—The International Music Products Association, and the National Academy of Recording Arts & Sciences (NARAS). The commission held a national symposium on music education in March 1991 in Washington, D.C. Leaders from education, government, business, and the arts participated in the symposium. The commission's final report of the symposium was Growing Up Complete: The Imperative for Music Education.

I'll tell you about a class I had...music appreciation. I didn't really think of it as a class, I thought of it as the period where we went and sang songs. We were learning that English precisely presents a writer's thoughts and feelings, that songs are a form of communication. We were learning history [through] the songs of the nation.... [It was] better than any other history class in my life. We were learning math, discovering the relationships between parts, and that composition followed mathematical rules. And we were learning to listen; if you don't listen you can't learn. This music appreciation connected my entire studies.

—Don Schlitz, songwriter, Testimony to the Commission, Nashville (November 14, 1990)

What is true of all the arts is supremely true of music. When a child studies music, significant elements of his or her education find focus and expression:

This chapter is reprinted from National Commission on Music Education, "Education with Music," *Growing Up Complete: The Imperative for Music Education* (Reston, VA: MENC, 1991). Copyright 1991 by MENC.

- developing the ability to understand and use symbols in new contexts;
- discovering the power, precision, and control of mathematics in unexpected ways;
- finding and directing personal creativity;
- exercising the diverse skills of problem-solving;
- experiencing the joy of self-expression;
- growing into the liberation acquired through self-discipline; and
- participating in the deeply human satisfaction of shared work and the gratification of challenges met.

In addition to these characteristics fundamental to education, music shares with the other arts a resource that is of paramount importance to

---

A Rationale for Music Education

Why should music be included as a basic part of the curriculum?

1. Music is worth knowing.
2. Music is one of the most important manifestations of our cultural heritage. Children need to know about Beethoven and Louis Armstrong as well as about Newton and Einstein.
3. Music is a potential in every individual that, like all potential, should be developed to its fullest.
4. Music provides an outlet for creativity, self-expression, and individual uniqueness. It enables us to express our noblest thoughts and feelings.
5. Music teaches students about unique aspects of their relationships with other human beings and with the world around them, in their own and other cultures.
6. Music opens avenues of success for students who may have problems in other areas of the curriculum and opens approaches to learning that can be applied in other contexts.
7. Studying music increases the satisfaction students derive from music by sharpening sensitivity, raising their level of appreciation, and expanding their musical horizons.
8. Music is one of the most powerful and profound symbol systems that exists.
9. Music helps students learn a significant lesson—that not all aspects of life are quantifiable.
10. Music exalts the human spirit.

Adapted from The School Music Program: Description and Standards, *Music Educators National Conference, 2nd ed., 1987* the education of the young: Music is a highway for exploring the emotional and aesthetic dimensions of experience. Indeed, here is where music and the other arts make their unique and most visible contribution. Education *without* music shortchanges our children and their futures. Education *with* music offers exciting possibilities in two directions. As we look to the future, educational research on the nature of intelligence and brain function give promising indications that could change the face of education. And as we look around us in the present, we see connections between music education and changes in students that offer direct and immediate benefits, not only to them, but to the educational enterprise as a whole.

Looking to the Future: Musical Intelligence

After nearly a decade of experience with the educational reform movement, policy makers are beginning to confront a disappointing truth: In terms of improving student achievement, not much has changed. We believe a new possibility is worth exploring. If music and the other arts were brought from the educational periphery to the core of learning, they could make a significant contribution to a more effective solution.

Music is beginning to be understood as a *form* of intelligence, not merely as a manifestation of it. The idea that intelligence is a single, monolithic entity or characteristic has been seriously questioned by many leading researchers and educators. Led by the provocative work of Howard Gardner, researchers and educators are moving toward a theory of "multiple intelligences," any or all of which can be developed.[1]

By "intelligence" Gardner means something like a distinguishable ability to solve and create different kinds of problems. His research identifies seven basic, *different* intelligences: linguistic, musical, logical-mathematical, spatial, bodily-kinesthetic, intra-personal (intelligence about one's own feeling life), inter-personal (intelligence about human interactions, temperaments, and motivations). Everyone has some capabilities in each of these; some intelligences are more dominant in some individuals than in others. Researchers continue to test the theory and work out the details, but Gardner's work helps us understand many aspects of learning and intelligence in a new and useful way.

Gardner's ideas are significant for the relationship of music education to general education. Since music is, for some learners, a powerful *way of knowing,* it can become, for teachers, a *way of teaching.* When important ideas, information, and ways of thinking can be approached through the strategies and structures provided by music, learning can be reinforced.

As the "way of knowing" present in musical intelligence is understood more comprehensively and applied to other kinds of learning tasks, music and music education may also hold the potential for tapping into underdeveloped abilities. In short, music may help children learn more, and more readily, beyond the limited contexts in which their musical intelligence is generally put to use. Gardner and his colleagues may have come up with a powerful, new argument for placing and keeping music at the core of the curriculum. Gardner's work offers us a new source of understanding from which to work. It is worth noting, however, that *at best, our educational system works diligently and systematically at developing only two of the seven intelligences* he identifies, the linguistic and the logical-mathematical. The other five are left to fend for themselves or find their nurture in the general culture.[2] Little wonder that American Federation of Teachers president Albert Shanker, a Commission member, has argued publicly that, at most, our schools do a good job with only 10 percent of our students. How could they do better when entire realms of individual human potential are slighted in the approach our schools take to education?

A "Window into the Brain"

Among the most fascinating witnesses heard by the Commission at its Los Angeles forum was Dr. Gordon Shaw, a physicist and brain researcher at the University of California–Irvine. According to Shaw, the 1990s will be the "decade of the brain." His own research focus is opening fruitful avenues into how the brain functions.[3]

Shaw's work has led him to posit that when the brain does certain tasks related to learning and memory, it reflects a structure that is, for all intents and purposes, "musical" in its form, shape, and timing. Using music, Shaw believes, we can examine higher creative and learning functions in new and potentially more productive ways.

Other scientists studying the brain report equally suggestive results, e.g., that the nature of music may have its roots in Nature itself. Richard Voss at IBM's Thomas J. Watson Center has found that nearly all music shares a simple mathematical formulation that expresses how notes change in pitch over the course of a musical work.[4] This same mathematical relationship is found in a wide variety of other natural patterns, including the changes in the electrical patterns of brain cells, the fluctuations of sunspots, and the growth of tree rings. The same mathematical formula that characterizes the ebb and flow of music exists widely in Nature, from the flow of the Nile to the beating of the human heart, to the wobbling of the earth on its axis. Voss's research reminds us of the ancient philosophers, who claimed that music is in harmony with the Cosmos itself. We are, it seems, "built" to learn, and where music offers a structural analogue to the learning process, it can and should be tapped into at the earliest possible age and used to the greatest possible extent. To ignore the significance of that for pedagogy would not only be foolish, it would be tragic.

Although the implications of these research results are still conjectural, if these investigations bear fruit, the possibilities for how we teach and learn are as exciting as they are profound. It is worth remembering that it has only been within the past generation that "left-brain/right-brain" discussion became commonplace in education, to the growing benefit of both instructional strategy and curriculum development. The consequences of denying the right brain's role in education was aptly pointed out to the Commission by music student Shirley Joo in Chicago, who likened it to "trying to climb a ladder with one leg."

Looking to the Present: Benefits to Students and All of Education

Beyond its intrinsic value, music education also opens the door to a number of utilitarian benefits. But a caveat is in order.

It would be enormously useful—but simplistic—to claim that music *causes* the benefits, e.g., self-esteem and self-discipline, with which it is so often associated by astute observers of children. From a strictly scientific point of view, however, such results have not been well demonstrated, for two reasons. One has to do with logic. Just because we can construct an association between two things does not mean that one produces the other (the rooster's crowing does not cause the sun to come up). The second reason is practical: While there is plenty of evidence that children who do well in music tend to do well at other things, it would take many

> ## A Teacher's Testimony
>
> *I have found, during my 18 years of teaching, that music students tend to score better on tests, have better communication skills, and are better disciplined students. They tend to be more prepared for the work force and are more readily hired by businesses. I have also seen several instances where music kept a student in school who would have otherwise dropped out.*
>
> —Jo Ann Hood, Music Teacher, Nashville Forum

studies with strict controls to demonstrate that the study of music alone produces these desired results.[5]

The Impact of Music at an Early Age

Nevertheless, where science cannot supply universal confidence, many studies are still instructive for understanding the impact of music education—*especially at an early age.* It is already abundantly clear, for instance, from the work done using the Orff, Suzuki, Yamaha, and Kodály methods of musical instruction—in this country and in Japan, Hungary, and elsewhere—that the musicality of preschool children can be translated into performance skills.

Reaching beyond music performance to other areas of learning, significant work has been done in Australia, where researchers have demonstrated statistically significant relationships between music instruction and positive performance in such areas as:

- reading comprehension, spelling, mathematics, and learning ability;[6]
- listening ability;[7]
- primary mental abilities (verbal, perceptual, number, and spatial);[8] and
- motor proficiency.[9]

Similarly, in this country, K–1 music instruction programs in the schools sponsored by Yamaha have been associated with remarkable achievement in reading. One study of the effects of the Yamaha program in the Downey, California, Unified School District showed, for example, that the reading level of first-grade students with a single year of music was nearly one grade higher than their peers; those with two years of music scored at almost the third-grade level; and some students scored as high as fourth- and fifth-grade levels.[10]

Early childhood exposure to music and music education can also have a significant impact on early child development. Dr. Frank R. Wilson, a neurologist and member of the Commission, together with music professor Franz Roehmann of the University of Colorado, organized an international conference on music and child development in 1987. One of the conclusions emerging from the conference was that "music has a profound influence on language [and] social and emotional maturation in children, beginning in infancy."[11] Edwin Gordon, at Temple University, has found that the earlier and more varied a child's music experiences, the greater the prospects for growth and development in music.[12] Wilson also notes that "as contemporary neurophysiology and psychomotor research discover more about the rhythmic organization of movement, it is likely that musical experience will be shown to have important effects on motor skills development as well."[13]

But we need not pile up scientific studies to show the nonmusical benefits of music education. Common sense lends support to the belief that music and music education foster a number of nonmusical factors important for success in school and life. Three areas are important here:

1. developmental goals such as self-esteem, self-discipline, and indi-

vidual creativity;

2. the development of important academic and personal skills; and

3. the contributions of music to other areas of study, particularly to their integration.

Music and Developmental Goals

Testimony from the music education community, as well as the verification of parents, teachers, and other adults, is almost universal in insisting that involvement in music powerfully encourages self-esteem, self-expression, creativity, and self-discipline.

Speaking to the Commission's Los Angeles forum, parent Pat Abicare reported seeing "first-hand" that "music and the other arts enable our students to build self-confidence through their ability to develop creativity and to find their freedom of expression." To enable her son to experience that, she was sending him to a school that was an 80-mile round-trip commute by school bus. Such stores are legion.

That music education contributes to these important developmental goals should come as no surprise. Correlations between successful performance and self-esteem, self-expression, and self-discipline exist in fields of endeavor that stretch across the curriculum and across life itself. When a child succeeds at such complex tasks as playing an instrument or singing

> *When my children were learning music in school, they had to learn other things; to sit still, to listen, to pay attention, to concentrate. With music you don't learn just music; you learn many things.*
> —Jackie Richmond, parent, Chicago Forum

in a chorus, self-esteem *is* enhanced.

When a child learns, by experience, that music forges direct links between self and world, self-expression becomes more fluent; the music helps interpret "who I am." The child who is taught how to create music is also learning something significant about his or her innate creativity. As a child begins to understand the connection between hours of practice and the quality of a performance, self-discipline becomes self-reinforcing. It is only a short jump from that realization to making the connection between self-discipline and performance in life.

Marion Etzel, a teacher educator at the Chicago Musical College of

Roosevelt University, spoke directly to the importance of music education among at-risk students at the Commission's Chicago forum. She reported that in the Chicago schools, where the overall school retention rate is 50 percent, one inner-city Hispanic school was able to boast a 95 percent retention rate, attributing its success in no small measure to its comprehensive music program.

It would be simplistic, of course, to suggest that music programs alone are the answer to significant educational and social problems among many of our youth. But it would be just as foolish to discount music education's contributions to finding solutions in these areas. Music is one of the few areas of study available to children that can bring such a diversity of positive factors together in the same classroom at the same time.

> *At perhaps no other time have music and arts education been more important. Apart from their obvious benefits, music and the other arts produce critical thinkers, people who are decision makers. In the information age, our company needs people with the critical thinking skills to analyze data and make judgments.*
> —Susan Driggers, Bell South Corporation, Nashville Forum

Music and Academic and Personal Skills

Music education also provides a critical introduction to and reinforcement of such academic and personal skills as critical thinking, problem-solving, and learning how to work cooperatively toward shared goals. Critical thinking skills are widely endorsed as a *sine qua non* for our children if they are to make much needed contributions to the work force. This requirement is being significantly affected by massive changes in the occupational structure of the work force.[14]

Of particular importance are skills acquired through learning how to manipulate symbols; higher order cognitive skills such as the ability to analyze, synthesize, and evaluate information; and the kinds of teamwork abilities and conflict-resolution skills required for success in the modern workplace.[15]

Such skills are both implicit and explicit in music instruction. The inherent mathematical underpinnings of music, for example, powerfully reinforce the analytical dimension of higher cognitive skills.

Abstract concepts such as counting, fractions, and ratios acquire concrete and tangible meaning when applied in musical context, and the relationships between symbol and context are much more readily made. Music requires the integration of eye-hand coordination, rhythm, tonality, symbol recognition and interpretation, attention span, and other factors that represent synthetic aspects of human intelligence. Moreover, the frequent requirement in music to subordinate individual performance to group goals, and the reinforcement music gives to the skills of cooperation, are among the qualities now most highly valued in business and industry, especially in high-tech contexts.

Music and Integration across the Curriculum

Many teachers have discovered that music can also be a powerful means of integrating other aspects of the curriculum. By tapping into the experiential and expressive aspects of music, teachers can add a distinctive dimension to instruction in other subjects. This insight has been used to develop interesting and productive pedagogical models like the Waldorf schools in Europe and the United States, and experimental instructional programs such as the Chelsea schools in Boston and at the Key School in Indianapolis, both of which are based on Gardner's theory of multiple intelligences.

These experimental approaches make use of music and the other arts in an educational program that seeks to decompartmentalize learning:

- In the Waldorf schools, for example, the goal is the education of the whole human being by paying attention to the needs of the human spirit. Art, music, and crafts all have the same weight as reading, writing, and arithmetic, in order to dissolve false dichotomies between school subjects. The arts, particularly, are used as part of a theory of human development that helps children find nonverbal modes of expression and understanding.
- In the Chelsea, Massachusetts, schools, music has been placed in the core of the curriculum in the belief that aesthetic development is critical to achieving other goals essential to education, among them reducing drop-out rates, increasing student attendance, improving self-esteem, teaching the importance of discipline, and producing culturally literate students. The aim, significantly, is to

change the ethos of the school system entirely, not merely to restructure or reorganize the curriculum.

- At the Key School, a public school in Indianapolis, principal Pat Bolaños reports a perspective similar to that of the Waldorf schools. "As a matter of equity," she says, "we stress all the intelligences."[16] All children take violin lessons in grades 1–3 before being able to branch out to other instruments. Thus the possibilities are greatly multiplied for identifying strengths in specific areas (like the arts) upon which to build instructional approaches. The arts are used to integrate across the curriculum, which is theme based rather than subject-area based.

Music Education and Self-Esteem

As we consider the difficult problems of inner-city schools and students there, we can readily see that music in the school may be the only beauty in the lives of some of these children.

In Sutro School in San Francisco, which has a large percentage of students with disadvantaged backgrounds, the problems of absenteeism, drop-outs, and lack of parental cooperation were rampant. The school created an opera— "Paddington Bear"—with the music and the libretto both created and performed by the children. I had the privilege of watching it.

After the bravos at the end of the performance, a group of us had the opportunity to meet with Julie Reinhoth, the principal. Someone asked her, "What did this do for the school?"

She said, "I can hardly begin to tell you. The youngster playing Paddington Bear was typical of our student body. Many of them have low self-esteem, many are shy, many are belligerent. Out of this program, many things have turned around. Students who could not work together have developed admirable patterns of cooperative behavior, better study habits, and higher achievement, both in and out of the classroom. Their self-esteem has grown by leaps and bounds. Parents have reached out to the school in a very helpful way. I could go on and on."

The children involved in this music program learned the self-discipline necessary to work harmoniously with others. They developed creativity, not only in writing the music and libretto, but also in building the sets, gathering the props, even learning to think on the spot during the performance, when someone forgot a prop and one of the other youngsters was able to improvise. They really learned to think on their feet.

—Norman Goldberg, president, MMB Music, Inc., Chicago Forum

Although participation in music education does not necessarily lead to improved academic performance in other subjects or across the board, there are impressive connections between participation in music classes and academic achievement. For example, in 1987–89, students taking music courses scored an average of 20 to 40 points higher on both verbal and math portions of the SATs than students who took no arts courses.[17]

Similarly, in a recent study the College Entrance Examination Board reported a direct correlation between improved SAT scores and the length of time spent studying six academic subjects, including "Arts and Music." Students with 20 units of study in the six areas scored 128 points higher on the SAT Verbal than those with 15 units; on the math portion, the difference was 118 points.[18] Students who took more than four years of music and the other arts scored 34 points better on verbal SATs and 18 points better on math SATs in 1987–89 than those who took music for less than one year.[19]

Music across the Curriculum

I have always felt that all the subjects are one and should be taught as one. I also feel that we should tell the kids this: It's all one, social studies, science, math, music.

I try to bring it to the level of their everyday life. One of the teachers was complaining about one of the band kids who was having a problem with fractions. She wanted to pull her from the band program. When I asked if the child could use any aids during the next exam, she said, "Calculators are out." I asked, "How about pie pans?" She gave me a strange look, but she said, "OK."

A long time before, I'd gone to one of the bakers in the city and he gave me a lot of pie pans. So when I teach the breakdown of music notation, it's the same thing as fractions, but, I teach it with the pie pans—a whole note is a whole pan, a half-note is half a pan, and so on. I told the math teacher, if you let this child take the test with the pie pans on her desk, she'll pass. She did, too. With an A.

—Mark Jordan, teacher, Samuel Gompers Elementary School, Chicago Forum

The contribution music and music education can make to the entire enterprise of learning for our children stands on firm ground. New research on intelligence and brain function point in exciting future directions that tie directly to music, while the continuing use of music as part of the curriculum is clearly associated with both academic skills and personal characteristics that are highly desirable for school progress and for developing the kind of well-educated young people we know we need for the nation's well-being. Music does not belong on the periphery but in the center.

Notes

1. See Howard Gardner, *Frames of Mind,* New York: Basic Books, 1983.

2. School sports may be a special case.

3. See X. Leng, G. L. Shaw, and E. L. Wright, "Coding Musical Structure and the Trion Model of Cortex," *Music Perception,* Vol. 8 (1990), pp. 49–62.

4. "The Musical Brain," *U.S. News & World Report,* June 6, 1990, pp. 56–62.

5. Among the most useful and comprehensive discussions of studies in this area is Karen Wolff, "The Nonmusical Outcomes of Music Education: A Review of the Literature," *Bulletin of the Council for Research in Music Education,* No. 55 (1978), pp. 1–27.

6. See G. F. Herbert, "The Nature of Teacher Training in the Implementation of a Development Programme of Music for the Primary School," *Music in Teacher Education: National Conference Report,* Melbourne: A.M.E.L., 1979, pp. 44–49.

7. See review of I. B. Tapley, "An Evaluation of Musical Training in Auditory Perception for First-grade Children," by J.T. Jetter, *Bulletin of the Council for Research in Music Education,* No. 61 (1980), pp. 50–55.

8. Anne Gates, "Extra-Musical Benefits of Music Education: Preliminary Investigation," Research report to the Australian-Japan Foundation (April 1980).

9. *Ibid.*

10. From the testimony of John Waltrip, president of Waltrip Music Centers of Arcadia, California, at the Commission's Los Angeles Forum, September 18, 1990.

11. See the Preface, *Music and Child Development,* Frank R. Wilson and Franz Roehmann, eds., St. Louis: MMB Music, 1990.

12. See Edwin Gordon, "The Nature and Description of Developmental and Stabilized Mental Aptitudes: Implications for Music Learning." *Ibid.,* pp. 325–35.

13. See Wilson and Roehmann, *loc. cit.* Commissioner Harold Smith, president of Baldwin Piano & Organ, notes that "in studying the piano, a child learns to read two lines of music, use both ears, both arms, fingers, legs, and feet," with the brain coordinating these multiple assignments simultaneously. See "Why Music Lessons Enhance a Child's Learning Power," *Music Trades,* October 1990, p. 92.

14. See Thomas Bailey, "Changes in the Nature and Structure of Work:

Implications for Skill Requirements and Skill Formation," in *Education and the Economy: Hard Questions, Hard Answers,* papers prepared for a conference on "Education and the Economy: Hard Questions, Hard Answers," sponsored by Teachers College, Columbia University, hels at Ocean Edge Conference Center, Brewster, Massachusetts, September 5–7, 1989, pp. 70–71.

15. See Sue E. Berryman, "What Do We Need to Teach? To Whom? When? How?" *Ibid.*, pp. 78–89.

16. Phone interview with Commission staff, December 12, 1990.

17. See "Data on Music Education: A National Review of Statistics," revised, compiled by Daniel V. Steinel, Music Educators National Conference, 1990, Table 4.3.

18. See "College Bound Seniors, The Class of 1990," College Entrance Examination Board, Princeton, NJ, August 28, 1990.

19. "Data on Music Education: A National Review of Statistics," Table 4.4.

The National Commission on Music Education was formed in 1990 under the sponsorship of MENC, NAMM—The International Music Products Association, and the National Academy of Recording Arts & Sciences.

Facing the Risks of the "Mozart Effect"

Bennett Reimer

Originally published as part of the Grand Masters series in the Music Educators Journal, *this article argues that music educators must protect the integrity of music education from alternative, nonmusic agendas. The implications of tying music study to outcomes such as mathematic achievement are fully discussed.*

Throughout its history in the United States, and in most countries and cultures around the world, the teaching and learning of music has been recognized as serving a variety of human needs. Some of these needs can be met only through music—that is, through the kinds of meanings and satisfactions that only musical sounds, defined and structured according to cultural expectations, traditions, and identity traits, can provide. Involvement with culturally significant musical events, through composing, improvising, performing, listening, or any other musical opportunities a culture provides, has been considered fulfilling to varying degrees, from the lightly entertaining to the profoundly spiritual. Teaching and learning music, then, have been understood to be valuable because they improve people's abilities to gain meaningful, gratifying musical experiences. Other needs served by studying music can also be valuable but can be fulfilled in a variety of ways not involving music or its study. Sometimes these other needs come into conflict with the musical ones. A glance backward in history will illustrate how this can happen.

Musical and Other Purposes of Music Education

Singing schools were established in the United States in the early eighteenth century to fulfill a need to improve the quality of singing as part of worship services—an important societal activity that depended on a higher level of musicality than that held by most members of the congregation. But in addition to fulfilling a musical need, these instructional

---

sessions were socially enjoyable for the people attending them. No doubt, some single individuals attended in the hope of meeting suitable partners (some things don't change over time). Also, the singing masters—the first professional music educators in the United States—were able, if they were successful, to make a decent living from the activity.

Singing schools, then, had the primary purpose of teaching music skills, while naturally and comfortably serving a variety of associated purposes. There were, of course, many other ways to enjoy companionship, to meet eligible partners, and to make a living. There was only one way, however, to satisfy the need for better singing—to learn how to sing better. The conflict occurred when several people who regularly attended a particular singing school began to complain that too much time and effort were being spent on singing instruction and that more time was needed for socializing, perhaps for potluck suppers, games, and so forth.

For the singing master—the music educator—this presented a dilemma. He (this was, then, a male role) was devoted to the musical task for which he was responsible and for which he had developed the necessary musical and pedagogical expertise. He had a course of study to deliver, including skills to develop, a musical repertoire to be studied, understandings to be nurtured, and learning assessments to be made; in short, he had a curriculum. But when he heard his students' complaints, he wondered if he was being too hard a taskmaster and needed to provide a bit more time for those other needs to be met. Or, perhaps, he should take the cue from his students' requests and make singing instruction secondary, devoting the most time and effort to the other, more social activities. Maybe he should go even farther, advertising his school as being focused on social and singles activities, thereby appealing to a wider constituency than those interested in learning to sing.

At what point would he be allowing the purpose of musical learning to become so altered by other purposes as to lose its centrality and veracity? At what point would the tail start wagging the dog? If he allowed this to happen, he might get more students in his classes and make more money. But what would that do to his professionalism, his musical self-respect, and his belief that musical values deserve a secure place in education, not to be displaced by other purposes that could be served just as well in other ways? Surely a wagging tail is a sign of a happy dog, so why not include appropriate attention to other values that add to the happiness of learning music? And why not even mention such values when justifying the need for and importance of his instruction? But how could he do so without weakening, or even sacrificing, the significant values that only music can impart? How could he protect the primacy of his music education curriculum?

The singing school master's dilemma has persisted over the centuries. If we fast forward now to the MENC National Biennial Conference in Phoenix, Arizona, in April 1998, we can hear Frances Rauscher, an experimental psychologist from the University of Wisconsin–Oshkosh, explaining her findings about the effects of music training on spatial-temporal reasoning. I, along with several hundred other music educators in a large room, listen intently. I am filled with mixed, conflicting thoughts and feelings.

On the one hand, my interests in musical intelligence, musical cognition, musical perceptual processing, musical learning mechanisms, and the like lead me to be extremely curious about how our brains process various stimuli, musical and otherwise, in ways we are only now beginning to investigate. A host of issues related to Rauscher's research arise in my mind, such as *reversibility*—whether direct training in spatial-temporal reasoning would positively affect musical perceptual responses; *experimental selectivity*—whether a variety of training regimens other than in music would produce even stronger effects than music did; *interaction effects*—what, precisely, in the experimental treatment actually caused the effects measured; *measurement*—how the measurement methodologies themselves influenced the findings, with other possible effects from a variety of interactions in musical learning going unnoticed; and *external validity*—whether professional performers, especially those steeped in the Western Classical tradition, have notably higher spatial-temporal reasoning levels or mathematical/scientific abilities than most other people. I find her work provocative as research, but I also see that it leads to important unanswered questions.

But it is another part of my response that ties me to my precursor colleague conducting a singing school. Over the centuries, from his time to ours, a great variety of human needs have aligned themselves with music teaching, usually quite compatibly and nonthreateningly. In most cases, music educators, despite their fears, have not been confronted with demands to so dilute their obligations to musical learning as to compromise their professional integrity. The troublesome scenario I envisioned for the singing master is unlikely to have occurred. Music educators generally have been able to attend to their primary purpose and be pleased that associated purposes are also served. But there has been a state of anxiety about the possibility that someday they might be pushed too far—that at some time, purposes other than musical ones might start to dominate, and, as individuals or collectively as a profession, they might have to stand up and be counted as supporters of the primary value of music.

As I sit there listening to Rauscher's presentation, I wonder, "Is this the time?" The unprecedented publicity given to her research and that of others on the effects of music on spatial-temporal mental functions, dubbed the "Mozart effect," has, ironically, placed the music education profession in a vulnerable position, perhaps more so than in any other such situation in its history. Spatial-temporal reasoning is thought to be foundational for success in higher mathematics, proportional reasoning (such as that used in engineering, structural design, architecture, and so forth), and other activities that require high mental ability (such as chess). These are high-stakes benefits, making others, such as opportunities to socialize and to meet partners, pale by comparison. Will music educators be placed in the position of having to justify music education on this new basis? If so, would they be held accountable to deliver the claimed spatial-temporal improvements? Would they, then, have to alter their curriculum of musical learnings in the direction of learnings most beneficial for developing spatial-temporal abilities? What would such a curriculum look like?

All these thoughts stream through my mind as Rauscher talks and as I recall listening to her on other occasions. At just about this point in my ruminations, I hear her say, "But I want to make something clear about the work I'm telling you about. It would be a terrible shame for music education to have to be justified on the basis of the kind of research I do and the kinds of findings I'm reporting." The entire audience bursts into spontaneous, enthusiastic applause. I am stunned by the intensity of feeling being expressed and am deeply moved by the message being given so powerfully—that music educators are devoted to *music* education and that they passionately and correctly insist that the tail, no matter how much clout it happens to have, must not wag the dog—the musical values and learnings to which they are dedicated.

The Vulnerability of Musical Values

The elation of that moment has passed, and I, along with many other music educators accustomed to being slightly paranoid, have reverted to my doubting ways. Sadly, these doubts have been fueled by an article in the *Arts Education Policy Review:* "Spatial-Temporal versus Language-Analytic Reasoning: The Role of Music Training" by Temple Grandin, Matthew Peterson, and Gordon L. Shaw.[1] This article, I am sorry to report, takes music educators perilously close to, if not over the edge of, the precipice they have long feared. Rauscher's comforting remark at the convention (noticeably absent from her articles) has been replaced (in this article co-authored by her frequent collaborator Gordon Shaw) by the clear, straightforward assertion that music's positive influence on spatial-temporal reasoning should be the purpose for music education.

The article begins with the claim that "recent experiments demonstrate that music can enhance reasoning . . . that specific music could enhance how we think, reason, and create."[2] Notice the assumption embedded in this claim—thinking, reasoning, and creating are mental functions absent in music, but they can be influenced by music. In an interview reported in the *Chicago Tribune,* Gordon Shaw states the following: "We're aware of the emotional impact of music. But we're saying it goes way beyond that. It has an effect on the reasoning and thinking part of the brain too."[3]

This assumption that music deals with emotion, which is separate and different from reasoning and thinking, is the legacy of the philosopher and mathematician René Descartes (1596–1650), whose enormously influential argument stated that mathematical thinking, conceived as being separate from involvement of the body and its unreliable senses and emotions, is the model for reasoning and for achieving pure intellect, which is reliable to the extent that it is abstract, free from the body and its emotions. This dualism separating mind and body has pervaded Western beliefs and education. It has led to the assumption that there are "intellectual" or "cognitive" subjects such as math, science, and languages that require intelligence and are therefore "basic" and that other subjects such as the arts, being rooted in the bodily senses and attendant emotions, are decidedly not "intellectual" or "cognitive," do not require intelligence, and are therefore not to be considered "basic." Spatial-temporal reasoning is a foundational component for certain of these "basic" subjects. If particular kinds of music and particular kinds of musical training improve such reasoning, then the case can be made that music should be included in education because of its positive effects on math, science, and other such learning, rather than for its own worth.

Over time, Descartes's ideas have been seriously questioned and in recent years have been directly contradicted. For example, in his book *Descartes' Error: Emotion, Reason, and the Human Brain,* neurologist Antonio Damasio asserts, "Contrary to traditional scientific opinion, feelings are just as cognitive as other percepts."[4] We have learned through recent scholarship that reasoning, thinking, creating, and "being cognitive" are not only deeply and necessarily pervaded with feeling, but that different domains of human endeavor require distinctive modes of reasoning, thinking, and creating—that these cognitive operations are manifested in domain-specific ways.[5] We are now beginning to understand that there is not a singular way to demonstrate intelligence but many ways in which humans are intelligent. Similarly, there is not a singular manifestation of creativity but many diverse ways of exhibiting it. Also, intelligence and creativity do not transfer automatically or readily from one area of knowledge to another: transfer is an arduous, uncertain task. Musical involvements *require* reasoning, thinking, creating, and cognizing—they require intelligences of the sort that various musical roles distinctively and characteristically enable humans to exhibit.

In the Grandin article, the authors report on several experiments designed to explore whether the pattern-recognition abilities necessary for musical processing would enhance these abilities for spatial-temporal reasoning. They explain why they chose the music of Mozart for the experiments: "We expected that Mozart . . . was exploiting the inherent repertoire of spatial-temporal firing patterns in the cortex in the ultimate manner. The particular sonata [K. 448] was carefully selected for its incredible use of the features of symmetry and natural sequences of patterns."[6] They report that a "causal link" was found between this music and spatial-temporal reasoning. Other kinds of music did not produce significant effects on spatial-temporal reasoning, but "future EEG [electroencephalograph] experiments might help predict which among different types of music would also produce the Mozart effect."[7] Private keyboard lessons produced highly significant improvement in a puzzle assembly task, but "no significant improvement was found on tests of spatial-recognition reasoning (such as matching, classifying, and recognizing similarities among objects)."[8] Astonishingly, this finding is completely ignored in the subsequent discussion.

The research studies reported in the Grandin article, and other studies related to them, require careful, exacting analysis because they raise a host of questions about their validity and credibility. Here, I want to deal with the conclusion that the article presents and its implications for music education. The article ends as follows:

> We strongly suggest that music education be present in our schools, preferably starting in preschool, to develop "hardware" for ST [spatial-temporal] reasoning in the child's brain. The absolutely crucial (but now neglected) role of spatial-temporal reasoning in learning different math and science concepts must be explored and exploited.[9]

I am going to take this conclusion directly and fully at its word. It says quite clearly that since spatial-temporal reasoning is crucial for math and science learning and since music has a positive effect on such reasoning, music education should be present in schools for the purpose of developing spatial-temporal "hardware" in students' brains. This perspective gives clear direction as to what an appropriate, relevant, valid, and successful program of musical studies should cover. To the degree that such a program enhances spatial-temporal reasoning, it will have both fulfilled the purpose of music education and have established its value in our schools.

Music educators are given an excellent opportunity here to explore the consequences of this popularly compelling and widely publicized rationale for music education, which is based on a distinctly different purpose than the development of people's abilities to gain significant, fulfilling experiences from music. The spatial-temporal rationale for music education is not simply another happy effect that happens to occur from a curriculum focused on musical learning. The argument based on the "Mozart effect" proposes that spatial-temporal reasoning development should be the point and purpose of music teaching in the schools. What, exactly, would this mean for music education?

The Implications

I want to suggest that the music education profession in the United States now has a practical and pertinent basis for answering the question of how the spatial-temporal rationale would alter music programs devoted to musical learning—the National Standards for Music Education.[10] To a very high degree, music educators have agreed that the nine content areas in the Standards should be the basis for all curricula in music, balanced to reflect various program emphases but with due attention to all of them. The profession has generally agreed that these nine content areas represent the fundamental ways in which music should be encountered and understood if it is to be incorporated into people's lives as comprehensively and meaningfully as possible. These areas constitute the knowledge base necessary for optimal musical experiencing.

Let's examine the Standards, reshaping them to fulfill the objective of music education as the spatial-temporal rationale conceives it.

The first two, dealing with singing and performing on instruments, are given clear direction from a spatial-temporal perspective. In one of the experiments, singing instruction was used as one of the controls, and it produced no improvements in spatial-temporal reasoning. This was disconcertingly camouflaged in the article in the observation: "There were three control groups of children, including a group receiving computer lessons. . . . The control groups did not improve significantly in any of the tests."[11] To the degree that this finding holds up in subsequent studies, singing could be safely eliminated from the music program. It would simply be irrelevant to spatial-temporal learning. If further research reverses this finding, we could reconsider it, but it is likely that a choice will have to be made between singing and performing on instruments, depending on which produces the stronger spatial-temporal effect.

As to performing on instruments, piano keyboard instruction, while producing mixed results as reported above, should be included because it does seem to effect spatial-temporal reasoning, at least as measured by puzzle manipulation. The piano instruction was in private lessons, so the "in groups" part of the standard ("alone and with others") is of doubtful utility and might have to be eliminated. And we are not at all certain about what, exactly, the children did that caused the one positive finding.[12] We know that the key elements related to spatial-temporal reasoning are "symmetry" and "natural sequences of patterns." Apparently Mozart's music from the Western classical period (roughly 1750–1820) demonstrates this inherent "naturalness." This implies that music from different periods and from other world cultures represents "unnatural" symmetries and sequences of patterns. So we would need to devise a regimen of symmetrical, sequentially patterned material in Western Classical style, which would be the basis for instruction. If future experiments did uncover other types of musical materials that would also produce the desired effect, then we could add them. The "varied repertoire of music" clause in the Standards clearly must be dropped because our program would include only those musical styles and types discovered to cause spatial-temporal improvement.

The question of which musical instruments to include is raised by the keyboard finding. It is likely that the spatial arrangement of keyboards is influential in effecting the results we seek. We would have to replicate the experiments to discover which other instruments, if any, produce similar improvements. We could then include instruction in any that produced the desired results. Further, it is not at all clear that musically expressive playing, as determined by each style of music being studied, has anything whatsoever to do with spatial-temporal reasoning. Nothing in the spatial-temporal research bears on this. Considering the enormous amount of time and effort that performance instruction spends on appropriate creative interpretation, including elements such as phrasing, balance, blend, dynamics, articulation, rhythmic fluency, melodic nuance, and so forth, we would be well served to eliminate as much of this as possible because most or all of it is likely to be irrelevant to the improvement of spatial-temporal reasoning.

Standard 3, dealing with improvisation, and Standard 4, dealing with composition, require experimental verification that they, in fact, improve spatial-temporal reasoning. At the moment, we know nothing about their efficacy for this purpose. Because they deal with musical materials in significantly different ways than performing composed music, students involved in improvising and composing are likely to demonstrate significantly different results on spatial-temporal reasoning measures. Computer composition is unlikely to be beneficial, given the negative results of the computer control group. It is possible that improvising on the keyboard with symmetrical patterns would be useful, but it is unlikely that composing at a keyboard will be fruitful for the purpose being pursued. For the moment, in the absence of evidence, it would be safe to hold improvisation and composition instruction in abeyance, awaiting research demonstrating that the musical intelligence and creativity that they call upon have significant effects on spatial-temporal functioning, as required for improved math and science learning.

Standard 5, dealing with reading and notating music, serves as an interesting case. Staff notation used for composing and performing Western music is highly spatial in orientation, including both vertical and horizontal spatial dimensions. Perhaps this accounted for at least some of the (partial) gains obtained. If so, we would need to intensify notation study, devising a variety of exercises exploiting the spatial framework in which staff notation operates. It may well be the case that notated, symmetrical, classical-style ("natural") pattern exercises, played on the piano keyboard, will be the key to the result being sought, producing the optimal spatial-temporal benefits from music education. Such exercises, indeed, may well prove to be more efficacious than Mozart's music itself, given the many nonsymmetrical, nonpatternlike aspects of his music, especially in his more expansive works such as the *Requiem Mass* and the operas, not to mention his later symphonies and chamber works. It is likely that we can eliminate all the nonessential musical material by depending on exercises based on the patterns and symmetries in the particular piano sonata that was used in this research as the stimulus, rather than actual pieces of music, thereby maximizing the desired effect on spatial-temporal reasoning.

This effect can be enhanced by Standard 6, which deals with listening to music. "Persistence of the EEG coherence patterns after listening to the Mozart sonata was observed for over twelve minutes."[13] Notice that this positive effect was produced with no musical instruction; subjects simply listened. Instruction about music for listening would perhaps be effective for spatial-temporal purposes if it were closely linked to playing and using notation as discussed above, but any other kind of listening-focused involvements, such as composing, improvising, analyzing, describing, and learning material from Standards 7, 8, and 9, (to be discussed shortly) would be highly questionable if not completely irrelevant.

In the *Chicago Tribune* interview to which I referred previously, Shaw was asked, "Have your findings changed your listening habits?" He replied, "Surely. I listen to a lot more Mozart."[14] He did not reply that he spent more time analyzing and describing Mozart's music or learning more about Mozart's life, the historical-cultural milieu from which he came, the musical heritage he built upon, the aesthetic posture he both adopted and expanded, his influences on music of his time and afterwards, the growth he exhibited as a musician and the inner and outer forces influential on it, or any other learning that is likely to provide the human context within which Mozart's music takes on dimensions of meaning that an intelligent listener both brings to and gains from the creative act of listening.

All that one needs to do to gain the desired effects, apparently, is listen. So, if we provided schools with a set of the appropriate recordings and asked that they be played at all possible times (especially immediately preceding math and science instruction), we would have fulfilled our obligation and would be relieved of any duties other than those requiring the playing/notation instruction so far discussed.

Standard 7 (having to do with evaluating music and music performance), Standard 8 (developing understandings about relationships between music, other arts, and other disciplines), and Standard 9 (understanding music in relation to history and culture) are all based on "language-analytic" reasoning. This kind of reasoning, according to Grandin, Peterson, and Shaw, is less desirable than spatial-temporal reasoning for learning math and proportional thinking; therefore, we cannot afford to waste precious time on it. Music educators are relieved of having to both learn such material themselves and teach it to their students, simplifying their work and their lives immensely. The new spatial-temporal reasoning justification would leave music educators with little to do as compared to the many challenges of the National Standards. But music educators would have the satisfaction of knowing that their radically redefined profession would be finally contributing to something "really useful," as compared to the trivial goal to which they have long been dedicated—enhancing musical experiences through more highly developed musical intelligences.

Reconciling Musical and Other Purposes

The spatial-temporal argument for the value of music study is perhaps the most extreme that the music education profession has ever faced. My analysis of this argument's logical consequences responds directly to its challenge. This forthright response is necessary, given the enormous promotion the "Mozart effect" has received and its imminent potential to force music education over the line that separates its devotion to musical learning, which the National Standards exemplify, and associated learning, which, rather than being comfortably assimilated within the Standards, becomes a replacement for them. It is very tempting for music educators, constantly in the position of having to justify the need for their subject in the schools, to regard a rationale such as improved spatial-temporal reasoning as a gift handed to them on a silver platter. But such a gift, as I have tried to demonstrate, is intended to serve only the purpose of the giver, not the receiver. There will be potentially destructive effects if the gift is accepted without a thorough examination of the consequences of accepting it.[15]

How can this unexpected, widely acclaimed benefit of music study be accepted without having it overwhelm musical values? Since the days of the singing school, the music education profession has managed to protect the primary purpose of music study from undue dominance by associated purposes. I would suggest that it can continue to achieve a proper balance through the following two responses.

First of all, music educators must not be rigid about their primary purpose of helping students better create and share the meanings and feelings that only music provides; they need not fear that this purpose is in danger of breaking apart when other interests are also accommodated. A purist, formalistic stance is not possible or desirable in the complex world in which music and music education exists. Music educators can recognize and even call attention to the many diverse benefits that music study offers without giving the impression, by their arguments or educational practices, that such benefits should ever threaten to replace their fundamental mission. By focusing on musical learning goals as stipulated in the Standards and graciously including a variety of purposes reflecting other interests, the profession can both protect the integrity of its musical responsibilities and comfortably serve a variety of associated values.

The key factor in maintaining an acceptable balance is the degree to which the program of musical learning is altered in order to serve other purposes, as my scenario in regard to the Standards in service of spatial-temporal reasoning illustrates. This kind of dangerous capitulation to other demands can best be deflected by agreeing that music study, such as we music education professionals are obliged to offer, can indeed make such contributions. We are happy that it has such positive effects, and as we go about fulfilling our musical teaching responsibilities, we will be sensitive to and supportive of all the many positive ways in which music study and experience can enhance people's lives.

Second, music educators must continue to learn about, apply, and conscientiously promote the benefits of involvements that are particular to music. As mentioned previously, work in cognitive science has clarified the fact that human knowing and intelligence are multifaceted and that various musical involvements provide opportunities to operate at the highest levels of cognition that humans are capable of—to understand, to create, and to share meanings as only music allows people to do and to exercise the intelligence particular to and dependent on each musical role. We have learned that musical doing, thinking, and feeling are essential ways in which humans make contact with, internalize, express, critique, and influence their cultural contexts. We know that musical teachings such as the Standards delineate are necessary if humans are to fully benefit from the opportunities and challenges their innate human capacities and their culture afford them. Such realizations deepen and strengthen the basis for musical learning as an essential component of education more securely, more convincingly, and more realistically than any others. Our expanding understandings of human knowledge, emotion, expression, and intelligence have solidified the essentiality of music to the human condition. The dog is very healthy. The obligation of the music education profession remains now, as in the past, to keep it so, and to be pleased that it wags its tail, as well.

Notes

1. Temple Grandin, Matthew Peterson, and Gordon L. Shaw, "Spatial-Temporal versus Language-Analytic Reasoning: The Role of Music Training," *Arts Education Policy Review* 99, no. 6 (July/August 1998): 11–14.

2. Ibid., 11.

3. Ronald Kotulak, "Q & A with Gordon L. Shaw," *Chicago Tribune*, May 24, 1998, sec. 2, p. 1.

4. Antonio Damasio, *Descartes' Error: Emotion, Reason, and the Human Brain* (New York: G. P. Putnam & Sons, 1994), xv.

5. The most influential argument of the domain specificity of intelligence is Howard Gardner, *Frames of Mind: A Theory of Multiple Intelligences* (New York: Basic Books, 1983).

6. Grandin, Peterson, and Shaw, "Spatial-Temporal versus Language-Analytic Reasoning," 12.

7. Ibid., 12.

8. Ibid., 13.

9. Ibid., 13.

10. MENC, *National Standards for Arts Education* (Reston, VA: MENC 1994).

11. Frances H. Rauscher et al., "Music Training Causes Long-Term Enhancement of Preschool Children's Reasoning," *Neurological Research* 19, no. 2 (1997): 3.

12. Ibid. The piano lessons were "traditional," including "pitch intervals, fine motor coordination, fingering techniques, sight-reading, music notation, and playing from memory."

13. Grandin, Peterson, and Shaw, "Spatial-Temporal versus Language-Analytic Reasoning," 12.

14. Kotulak, "Q & A with Gordon L. Shaw," 3.

15. For a parallel discussion of threats to arts education from claims of effects on improved performance in the "academic" subjects, see Elliot Eisner, "Does Experience in the Arts Boost Academic Achievement?" *Art Education* 51, no. 1 (January 1998): 32–38.

Bennett Reimer is professor of music education emeritus in the School of Music at Northwestern University in Evanston, Illinois.

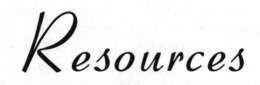

Resources

Annotated Bibliography: Music, Brain Development, and Learning

Wendy L. Sims and Cathi C. Wilson

This listing includes resources in three categories: data-based research published in scientific or psychological journals, articles in professional journals, and articles in the popular press. Under the data-based research journals, readers will find brief summaries of each article.

The potentially positive relationships among music, the brain, and learning have been the focus of much media attention since the mid-1990s. A body of literature is beginning to be developed in this area, including research studies, philosophical discourses and debates, and articles in education journals and the popular press. At this point, however, it is too soon to determine whether listening to, studying, or performing music results in temporary or permanent changes in the brain and whether music-related changes in the brain result in generalizable changes in cognitive processing or development. Much more physiological, behavioral, and longitudinal research is needed before it may be claimed that music really does have a meaningful, positive effect on brain development.

One of the related, controversial issues is the extent to which "music makes you smarter" should be used in advocacy for school music programs. Music educators will certainly be as thrilled as anyone if music is proven to have real, long-lasting, and valuable learning benefits for children. Many of us actually believe in our hearts that this may be true. It is premature to make these claims based on the small amount of research data available currently, however. Music activities can be used to meet many objectives and educational needs of children in almost every curricular and cocurricular area imaginable, in ways that are very motivating and interesting to the children. These are worthy, valuable, and important uses of music. But, most music educators also believe passionately that music should be taught because it is an intrinsically valuable subject matter.

It is not easy to reconcile the need for strong advocacy for music programs with the caution expressed by many in our research community against over-generalizing research results. The best approach may be one of cautious optimism—music listening or study may indeed enhance cognitive development, it will certainly do no harm, and it undoubtably will enhance musical development!

The Bibliography

MENC—The National Association for Music Education has received numerous requests for information about this topic. This bibliography will allow interested parties to find, read, and assess for themselves research and other articles related to music, the brain, and music learning. Articles were selected based on their pertinence to the topic, accessibility, and recency (past 5 years only, since the term "Mozart Effect" became part of the popular vocabulary—for earlier work, refer to the articles' bibliographies). While we attempted to include all articles meeting these criteria, research in this area is proliferating rapidly, and any omissions are neither intentional nor statements on the quality of the work omitted. In the case of data-based research, primarily articles that have passed through the stringent peer-review process required for publication in professional journals have been included (with the exception of the 1994 conference paper that spawned the current interest in this topic, as well as some related "scientific correspondence").

The bibliography is categorized by type of entry:
- Data-based research published in scientific or psychological journals—articles that are very academic and technical in nature
- Articles in professional journals—articles that are less technical and more practical, drawing on research and theory to inform practice
- Articles in the popular press—a sample of reports from outside academe
- Websites—internet addresses for directly related sites

Within each category, entries appear in chronological order.

Data-Based Research Published in Scientific or Psychological Journals

The annotations provided for each article in this category are designed to provide some basic information about the article's content, to assist readers in deciding whether they want to obtain a copy of the full article. Information contained in these brief annotations should not be used under any circumstances as a substitute for the original, primary source.

Rauscher, F. H., Shaw, G. L., Levine, L. J., Ky, K. N., & Wright, E. L. (1994, August). Music and spatial task performance: A causal relationship. Paper presented at the meeting of the American Psychological Association 102nd Annual Convention, Los Angeles, CA.

Data from two studies are presented. The first found that college students' spatial-temporal reasoning ability was affected positively by listening to music by Mozart, but not to music characterized as minimalist/rhythmically repetitive. The second study of 37 three-year-old children found that children in the group receiving weekly keyboard and daily singing lessons for 8 months demonstrated significant improvement on a spatial-temporal task as compared with children who did not participate in music lessons.

Elbert, T., Pantev, C., Wienbruch, C., Rockstroh, B., & Taub, E. (1995). Increased cortical representation of the fingers of the left hand in string players. *Science, 270*, 305–07.

"Magnetic source imaging revealed that the cortical representation of the digits of the left hand of string players was larger than that in controls. . . . Results suggest that the representation of different parts of the body in the primary somatosensory cortex of humans depends on use and changes to conform to the current needs and experiences of the individual." (p. 305)

Schlaug, G., Jancke, L., Huang, Y., & Steinmetz, H. (1995). In vivo evidence of structural brain asymmetry in musicians. *Science, 267*, 699–701.

Results of *in vivo* magnetic resonance morphometry of the area of the brain called the planum temporale indicated that "musicians with perfect pitch revealed stronger leftward planum temporale asymmetry than nonmusicians or musicians without perfect pitch. The results indicate that outstanding musical ability is associated with increased leftward asymmetry of cortex subserving music-related functions." (p. 699)

Rauscher, F. H., Shaw, G. L., & Ky, K. N. (1995). Listening to Mozart enhances spatial-temporal reasoning: Towards a neurophysiological basis. *Neuroscience Letters, 185*, (1), 44–47.

The results of this experiment replicate the authors' previous work, that listening to a Mozart piano sonata "produced significant short-term enhancement of spatial-temporal reasoning in college students." This demonstrated that (i) repetitive music does not enhance reasoning; (ii) a taped short story does not enhance reasoning; and (iii) short-term memory is not enhanced. (p. 44)

Rauscher, F. H., Shaw, G. L., Levine, L. J., Wright, E. L., Dennis, W. R., & Newcomb, R. L. (1997). Music training causes long-term enhancement of preschool childrens' spatial-temporal reasoning. *Neurological Research, 19* (1), 2–8.

Significant improvement on a spatial-temporal test was found for a group of 34 preschool children receiving private piano lessons for six months. This was not true for students receiving private computer lessons or a control group. No effect was found on spatial recognition tests for any group.

Sarnthein, J., von Stein, A., Rappelsberger, P., Petsche, H., Rauscher, F. R., & Shaw, G. L. (1997) Persistent patterns of brain activity: An EEG coherence study of the positive effect of music on spatial-temporal reasoning. *Neurological Research, 19* (2), 107–116.

The authors suggest that the electroencephalogram (EEG) coherence results they found "provide the beginnings of understanding of the neurophysiological basis of the causal enhancement of spatial-temporal reasoning by listening to specific music." (p. 107).

Wilson, T. L., & Brown, T. L. (1997). Reexamination of the effect of Mozart's music on spatial-task performance. *Journal of Psychology, 131*, (4), 365–370.

College students who listened to 10 minutes of Mozart completed more paper and pencil mazes (a spatial reasoning task) in the time allotted, with fewer errors, than students listening to relaxation music or silence. Students who listened to relaxation music performed better than those who experienced silence.

Gromko, J. E., & Poorman, A. S. (1998). The effect of music training on preschoolers' spatial-temporal task performance. *Journal of Research in Music Education, 46* (2), 173–181.

Preschool children were assessed on five spatial-temporal tasks after receiving either weekly music instruction including playing songbells, or no treatment (control group), for eight months. Results indicated that the treatment group "showed a significantly higher mean gain on [the assessment] and that the gain held steady across ages within the treatment group" (p. 178). The authors conclude that "music training can have a positive effect on the development of spatial intelligence in preschool children" (p. 178).

Pantev, C., Oostenveld, R., Engelien, A., Ross, B., Roberts, L., & Hoke, M. (1998). Increased auditory cortical representation in musicians. *Nature, 392*, 811–814.

The results of this study, which compared magnetic fields evoked in the brain by piano tones, "raise the possibility that musical experience during childhood may influence structural development of the auditory cortex." (p. 813).

Rauscher, F. H., & Shaw, G. L. (1998). Key components of the Mozart effect. *Perceptual and Motor Skills, 86*, 835–841.

This paper discusses the results of a number of studies designed to replicate the authors' previous findings that listening to Mozart enhanced spatial-temporal reasoning. The authors conclude that discrepancies among results may be attributable to differences in task validity, experimental design, subjects' age, musical training, preferences, and aptitude for the task (p. 839).

Graziano, A. B., Peterson, M., & Shaw, G. L. (1999). Enhanced learning of proportional math through music training and spatial-temporal training. *Neurological Research, 21* (2), 137–152.

Second-grade children from disadvantaged backgrounds participated in an experiment to compare the effects of piano keyboard lessons paired with a math computer game, English lessons paired with the math game, and no lessons on spatial-temporal reasoning, fractions and proportional math. Results indicated children in the group receiving the piano lessons plus math game scored significantly higher on proportional math and fractions than the children in the English lessons plus math game group. The authors present several reasons why music may enhance spatial-temporal reasoning.

Scientific Correspondence: Prelude or requiem for the "Mozart effect"? (1999) *Nature, 400*, 826–828.

Submissions by C. F. Chabris and K. M. Steele et. al. present short descriptions of research they have completed that dispute the finding that listening to Mozart results in differential improvement in spatial reasoning. A rebuttal by F. H. Rauscher, one of the authors of the research being questioned, is included.

Costa-Giomi, E. (1999). The effects of three years of piano instruction on children's cognitive development. *Journal of Research in Music Education, 47*, 198–212.

Cognitive abilities of children who were provided with individual piano lessons from fourth through sixth grade were compared with children who were not provided with lessons. There was a small effect on the general and spatial cognitive abilities of children receiving lessons, and no effect on the development of quantitative and verbal cognitive abilities. "Additional analyses showed that although the experimental group obtained higher spatial abilities scores in the Developing Cognitive Abilities Test after 1 and 2 years of instruction than did the control group, the groups did not differ in general or specific cognitive abilities after 3 years of instruction" (p. 198).

Articles in Professional Journals

The articles in this category will not be annotated individually. All of the articles discuss the research and its implications or applications for music education. Unlike the single-focused, data-based research articles summarized above, it would be very difficult to capture the essence of these articles in a few sentences. The titles do provide good general descriptors of the articles' contents, however.

Snyder, N. (interviewer) (1995). Frances Rauscher: Music and reasoning. *Teaching Music, 2* (5), 40–41, 50.

Black, S. (1997). The Musical Mind. *The American School Board Journal, 184* (1), 20–22.

Lehr, M. R. (1998). Music Education: The Brain-building subject. *Teaching Music, 6* (3), 40, 56.

Overy, K. (1998). Discussion Note: Can music really "improve" the mind? *Psychology of Music, 26,* 97–99.

Rauscher, F. H., Spychiger, M., Lamont, A., Mills, J., Waters, A. J., & Gruhn, W. (1998). Responses to Katie Overy's paper, "Can music really 'improve' the mind?" *Psychology of Music, 26,* 197–210.

Green, F. E. (1999). Brain and learning research: Implications for meeting the needs of diverse learners. *Education, 119* (4), 682–687, 681.

Barrett, C.M. (1998). New brain research and the Suzuki method. *American Suzuki Journal, 26* (4), 39–41, 43.

Eisner, E. W. (1998). *Does experience in the arts boost academic achievement?* [Brochure]. Reston, VA: National Art Education Association.

Grandin, T., Peterson, M., & Shaw, G. L. (1998). Spatial-temporal versus language-analytic reasoning: The role of music training. *Arts Education Policy Review, 99* (6), 11–14.

Viadero, D. (1998, April 8). Music on the mind. *Education Week, 17* (30), 25–27.

Weinberger, N. (1998). Brain, behavior, biology, and music: Some research findings and their implications for educational policy. *Arts Education Policy Review, 99,* 28–36.

Flohr, J.W. (1999). Recent brain research on young children. *Teaching Music, 6* (6), 41–43, 54.

Reimer, B. (1999). Facing the risks of the Mozart effect. *Music Educators Journal, 86* (1), 37–43.

Wilcox, E. (1999). Straight Talk about Music and Brain Research. *Teaching Music, 7* (3), 29–35.

Articles in the Popular Press (articles may be available via archives on the publications' Web sites)

This list is a mere sample of the types of articles published in the national media dealing with the issues and controversies surrounding music, the brain, and learning. The articles in this category will not be annotated individually—their titles speak for themselves.

Elias, M. (1994, August 15). Music lessons may open mind to math, science. *USA Today,* 1D.

Begley, S. (1996, February 19). Your child's brain. *Newsweek,* 127 (8), 54–59, 61–62.

Elias, M. (1996, May 23). Singing class helps math, reading skills. *USA Today,* 8D.

Pouliot, J. S. (1996, May/June). Music for the mind. *Correspondent,* 24–25.

Kupferberg, H. (1999, February 28). The new sounds of success in school. *Parade,* 8–9.

Mulhammad, L. (1999, March 15). Piano training is a noteworthy math teaching tool. *USA Today,* 1D.

Marsh, A. (1999, April 19). Can you hum your way to math genius? *Forbes,* 176, 178, 180.

Goode, E. (1999, August 3). Mozart for baby? Some say, maybe not. *The New York Times,* F1, F9.

Web sites

These two Web sites are sources for current information and scientific research related to music and the brain.

MuSICA, the Music and Science Information Computer Archive—www.musica.uci.edu

---

This site provides a bibliographic database, research notes, news, notices, funding sources, and other related items of interest.

MIND (Music Intelligence Neural Development) Institute—www.mindinst.org

According to this Web site, MIND is "a basic science research institute with the primary goal of understanding the neural machinery of higher brain function in order to advance education and medicine." The site includes research summaries, bibliographies and information about publications, and frequently asked questions.

Wendy L. Sims is professor and director of music education at the University of Missouri–Columbia (UMC), and Cathi C. Wilson is a graduate student at UMC.

Web Sites

Sue Rarus

MENC's Information Services office compiles information and data for use by music teachers and supporters of music education. This listing includes current Web sites with content related to music.

The American Music Conference: Contains information on music and learning, the national standards for music, general music resources and links, and several links to music research databases.

> www.amc-music.com/pages/research/index.html

Arts Education Partnership: This site highlights several current arts in education projects. Case studies from around the country show how the integration of the arts into the curriculum can make a difference.

> http://aep-arts.org

Childrens' Music Workshop: Music Education OnLine-A Guide to Music Education for Gr. K–12 This site links to a plethora of information and research, all categorized by topic: "The Mozart Effect and Enhanced Intelligence," "Music, Memory and Learning," "Nurture vs. Nature," and so forth. Easily accessible and understandable. Useful factoids.

> www.childrensmusicworkshop.com

Harvard Project Zero: The Project Zero home page provides a useful overview of this research project, which resides at the Harvard Graduate School of Education. Project Zero's focus is on understanding the processes of thinking, learning, and creativity in the arts, at both the individual and institutional levels. Much work has been done at Project Zero regarding the theory of multiple intelligences, of which music is considered to be one. Project Zero's work empirically contextualizes the debate on the arts and learning.

> http://pzweb.harvard.edu

Institute for Music Research: This site, from the University of Texas at San Antonio, contains research information on music and learning, and highlights the Computer Assisted Information Retrieval Service System (CAIRSS), which is a bibliographic database of music research literature in music education, music psychology, music therapy, and music medicine. Citations from 1,354 different journal titles.

> http://imr.utsa.edu/CAIRSS.html

International Foundation for Music Research: Research guide. News and events. Publications. Grants and funding. Research tools. Links to MuSICA: Music and Science Information Computer Archive and other research sites.

http://www.music-research.org

The International Society for Music Education: The multiple references on this site provide an international perspective on teaching music, music education, and research in music. ISME is based at the University of Reading in the U.K. and originated in 1953 as an outgrowth of a UNESCO sponsored conference to "stimulate music education as an integral part of general education." The global viewpoints available on this site make it a particularly worthwhile resource for any music educator, as he or she works with an increasingly multicultural student population.

www.isme.org/findex.html

MMB Music—On-line Education Resources: A wonderfully diverse list of music education resources.

www.mmbmusic.com/mused_links.html

The Music and Science Information Computer Archive: MuSICA originates from the University of California, Irvine. This site contains a bibliographic database of scientific research on music as it relates to behavior, the brain, and related fields. It also contains *MuSICA Research Notes,* a newsletter issued three times a year that reports on and gives analysis of music and behavior.

www.musica.uci.edu/

The MUSIC Education Resource Base: A bibliographic database of more than 30,000 resources in music and music education from 32 Canadian and international journals, and from other sources, covering the period 1956 through today. The journals are fully indexed by title, author, and subject. The database is searchable and maintained in part by a grant from the McPherson Library at the University of Victoria, Calgary, Canada.

www.ffa.ucalgary.ca/merb

Music Education Resource Links (MERL): This site originates from the University of the Pacific School of Education. It provides links to sites which provide content for the National Standards for Arts Education, as well as other links on a variety of music-related subjects.

www.cs.uop.edu/~cpiper/musiced.html

The Music Education Search System: Two databases containing information regarding music teaching and learning. The music journal database contains more than 12,000 bibliographic entries for articles contained in a dozen or so highly regarded music journals, and the Poland-Cady Abstract Collection contains over 4,500 entries regarding music research, pre-1966. (Also found on the NEA site at www.arts.endow.gov/artforms/Music/Music6.html)

> http://www.music.utah.edu/research/musicRsrch.html

National Music Education Coalition Website: A website containing information drawn from material supplied by MENC: The National Association for Music Education and NAMM: The International Music Products Association to provide advocacy information and tools that support the existence of strong music education programs in American schools.

> http://www.supportmusic.com

Research Perspectives in Music Education: The *Research Perspectives* is published under the auspices of the School of Music at the University of Southern Florida. Subscription information is available on line. The site contains a variety of research articles written by professionals working in the field of music education.

> www.arts.usf.edu/music/rpme.html

The Saguaro Seminar on Civic Engagement in America: This site, sponsored by the John F. Kennedy School of Government at Harvard University, provides excerpts from an on-going discussion of experts on various aspects of civic involvement in the U.S. Seminar #7 discusses the effects of the arts in society. This site gives a description of the issues and ideas around which the discussion centered. The complete recommendations from this seminar should be out in late Spring of 2000.

> http://www.ksg.harvard.edu/saguaro/mtg7.html

The WORLDWIDE Internet Music Resources: A site of the Indiana University School of Music, offered as a service of the William and Gayle Cook Music Library, Indiana University. Topics covered include, but are not limited to, Genres and Types of Music; Research and Study; the Commercial World of Music; Journals and Magazines, Composers and Composition.

> www.music.indiana.edu/music-resources/

Sue Rarus is information services manager at MENC—The National Association for Music Education.
